Latin Dance

Recent Title in
The American Dance Floor

Country & Western Dance
Ralph G. Giordano

Latin Dance

Elizabeth Drake-Boyt

The American Dance Floor
Ralph G. Giordano, Series Editor

AN IMPRINT OF ABC-CLIO, LLC
Santa Barbara, California • Denver, Colorado • Oxford, England

Library of Congress Cataloging-in-Publication Data

Drake-Boyt, Elizabeth.
  Latin dance / Elizabeth Drake-Boyt.
    p. cm. — (The american dance floor)
Includes bibliographical references and index.
ISBN 978–0–313–37608–5 (hard copy : alk. paper) — ISBN 978–0–313–37609–2 (e-book)
1. Dance—Latin America. I. Title.
GV1626.D73   2011
793.3'19098—dc22   2010043781

ISBN: 978–0–313–37608–5
EISBN: 978–0–313–37609–2

15 14 13 12 11   1 2 3 4 5

This book is also available on the World Wide Web as an eBook.
Visit www.abc-clio.com for details.

Greenwood
An Imprint of ABC-CLIO, LLC

ABC-CLIO, LLC
130 Cremona Drive, P.O. Box 1911
Santa Barbara, California 93116-1911

This book is printed on acid-free paper ∞

Manufactured in the United States of America

Contents

Series Foreword

From the Lindy hop to hip-hop, dance has helped define American life and culture. In good times and bad, people have turned to dance to escape their troubles, get out, and have a good time. From high school proms to weddings and other occasions, dance creates some of our most memorable personal moments. It is also big business, with schools, competitions, and dance halls bringing in people and their dollars each year. And as America has changed, so, too, has dance. The story of dance is very much the story of America. Dance routines are featured in movies, television, and videos; dance styles and techniques reflect shifting values and attitudes toward relationships; and dance performers and their costumes reveal changing thoughts about race, class, gender, and other topics. Written for students and general readers, *The American Dance Floor* series covers the history of social dancing in America.

Each volume in the series looks at a particular type of dance such as swing, disco, Latin, folk dancing, hip-hop, ballroom, and country & western. Written in an engaging manner, each book tells the story of a particular dance form and places it in its historical, social, and cultural context. Thus each title helps the reader learn not only about a particular dance form but also about social change. The volumes are fully documented, and each contains a bibliography of print and electronic resources for further reading.

Preface

Nothing that happened while I was growing up prepared me to be an expert on Latin dances. Although Spanish was sometimes spoken in my home, it was incidental because my mother had spent some of her teen years in Mexico. She spoke it only with her friend Maria, because Bill Medina, who came out to our Iowa farm to help with the work, had married Maria in Mexico and brought her back with him to live in Des Moines. Maria didn't speak English at the time, and Mother was the only one she knew who spoke Spanish. So Maria was often at our farm, too; she taught me how to make sweet tamales and how to dance. Through Maria, I got an early taste of sweet tamales (corn mixed with sugar, raisins, and cinnamon) as well as the hot in my mouth, all-night doses of conjunto music in my ear, and a way of moving that went through the body and into the earth itself. Even with this kind of start, my trail to Latin dances was as long and winding as a conga line.

I love to dance. It has always been—since the moment I could walk—and always will be, my greatest joy in life. And in my world at that time, only one word encompassed the lofty goal of becoming a dancer: ballet.

As the only girl among four younger brothers, I had many "critics" of my dance creativity. Any "Latin motion" dancing was especially commented upon, and jibes from the "all-male peanut gallery" suggesting I take up belly dancing froze my core. Well, there were ways around that. Not all dancing had to have hip moves and the sexual connotations that went along with that. I took ballet and classical

Spanish dances as taught by Elizabeth Werblosky in Des Moines, Iowa. A fiery, petite lady, "Miss Elizabeth" despaired of my ever being able to manage the multiple turns, changes of direction, and rhythmic response that any respectable dancer should have. So she patiently taught me as much as she could from the Spanish dances that her own teacher, Cansino (who also taught his daughter, Rita Hayworth), had passed on to her. I was very happy with that. No Latin motion, and no swinging hips suggesting sex of any kind in ballet or these Spanish dances. Now, if only I could get my fingers to articulate the castanets, I'd have it made.

Only, I never did quite make it. All that work did improve rhythmic response, but not enough to really go beyond perpetual amateur status. A huge gap fell between my abilities and my dancing ambitions. I was pretty stiff from riding horses, and age fifteen was late to start learning. I knew it wasn't going to be easy; I just never considered the possibility that it might be impossible. And I didn't give up.

While I worked at it, I read about dance and viewed every live performance, film, or TV show that had any dance in it. All kinds of dance, all over the world; wherever and whenever music played and dancers moved. I traveled a lot, and where I went, I recorded dances—some of which have since disappeared—that I saw in journals. I kept taking dancing lessons in the midst of raising two children and frequent moves with a husband in metallurgical engineering. I not only studied jazz and tap but also dance-like activities such as Tai Chi, stage combat techniques, Chinese wand exercise, and even foil fencing—for which I became a practice judge. But a frozen core (not to mention knees and ankles that don't flex well) did not help, and my whole idea of dance was to get off the ground, not sink to it.

When I took classes in modern dance at the University of Arizona from two fabulous teachers, I was the oldest student in the class. But I finally learned that gravity wasn't the enemy of expressive movement, and that the earth itself offers the strength of self-empowerment. And later, one of my professors at Florida State University, Dr. Anita Gonzalez, who is also a founding member of Urban Bush Women, took me with her on a research trip to visit these dance performers. There I began to understand how drummers and dancers "talk" to each other. I fell in with my neighbors, who were from all over the world—especially the wives of students from Egypt and Turkey. These Muslim ladies danced—hour upon hour—safe and secure from the eyes (and jokes) of men, and I joined them until 9/11 struck, and it was no longer safe for us to dance together. But things inside my core had started to rattle.

Finally, another professor took me to a conference in New Orleans where we found a family-friendly zydeco spot, and somehow, with that same encouragement of inclusion, I managed to learn the Cajun two-step, gliding waltz, and the joyful zydeco, hitting that off-beat "limp" shoulder to shoulder with the best of them. I couldn't get enough of it. We stayed so long into the night, sailing along to fiddle and accordion, that the frottoir player gave up, strapped me into the washboard, and handed me the spoons.

Well, that certainly was the beginning of the end, and better late than never! Ever since, I've looked for opportunities to try out just about every Latin dance I could find. True, capoeira and breaking will probably not be at the top of my list, but then again, you never know. So when one of my esteemed dance history associates (who had also been one of my professors) let me know that Ralph Giordano was looking for writers for the Greenwood American Dance Floor series, I raised my hand at once, delighted to be assigned the Latin social dances (even though I really, truly am not any kind of an expert on them). After all, I still have a lot to learn.

Acknowledgments

I would like to extend my grateful appreciation to everyone who guided me through the process of writing this book. Certainly Series Editor Ralph Giordano deserves my heartfelt thanks for guiding the process start to finish and keeping me on track. Editors Erin Ryan and George Butler at ABC-CLIO, LLC have been invaluable help in shaping the content, finding images, and putting the book in good form. Without them, this project would certainly not have been possible. I would also like to commend the Kentucky Daviess County Public Library staff, with whose help I was able to access excellent materials in support of my research. Thanks also go to photographers Jack Crockett and Allen Spatz for providing some of the excellent images that help tell the story of Latin social dancing in the United States.

My long-suffering family also deserves abundant credit for patiently enduring my absence during the time that my efforts were devoted to the project, especially husband Charly, who continually interrupted his own writing projects to sympathize with every setback or cheer each step of progress—not to mention his invaluable help with line editing. I offer him affectionate gratitude.

Introduction

[Salsa is] a little animal that gets into your eyes and ears, and when it reaches your heart, it bursts out and you can't avoid it.

Celia Cruz[1]

It is no exaggeration to say that Latin dances are among the most popular of social dances anywhere in the world. They are found everywhere and in all dance venues, from serious concert art dance performances (ballet and modern) to neighbors' patio parties and the hottest clubs in every major city of the United States. Indispensible to exhibition and DanceSport competition, Latin dances are the ultimate expression of couples' social dancing in the United States, as they allow dancers to explore the rich complexity of balances of power and pleasure in pairs; one to lead, and the other to follow. From the sudden intensity of tango corté figures to the snappy, sassy whip-steps and rolling pelvis of salsa, a dancing pair expresses relationship emotions in all degrees; attraction, combat, flirtation, betrayal, rejection, longing, desire, passion, and fantasy.

But couples aren't the only ones to enjoy Latin dancing. There is an almost inexhaustible variety of configurations possible on the Latin social dance floor. From celebratory conga lines to casino rueda wheels, to zumba classrooms filled with exercise enthusiasts to individual displays of virtuoso partnering in mambo or capoeira, Latin dances are one-on-one as well as one-to-many. And other social dance

Dancer Erin Boyt embodies the regal bearing and sensual romanticism of Spanish Latin dances. (© Jack Crockett. Used by permission.)

styles pick up a note of drama when touched with that unmistakable Latin rhythm and style. In their social forms (as opposed to exhibition and/or competition variants), Latin dances are infinitely inclusive; the basic steps are generally easy to learn in a few lessons, yet take a lifetime of study to master. They accommodate a broad range of physical and mental conditions; even wheelchair. Though each Latin dance has its own rhythmic and melodic signature, there is in every one the opportunity to improvise within the form. And all of them are held together by the inescapable "key," or clave five-count beat that is at the heart of Latin music.

Latin dances are about power and the survival of identity in the unimaginably harsh conditions of slavery and immigration. They provide the space where identity and origin are proclaimed in a salsa, depending on whether or not the dancer steps out on the first beat.[2] The history of how these dances were brought onto dance floors in the United States is one bordered by racism. While media and mass culture representations told the "tamed" part of the story, another part flowed under it like an underground stream—parallel but not visible—that is, until Latin began to dance with African-American jazz and together they made the big time in the recording industry.

The politics of Latin dances continue to change—from Hollywood's early caricature of them (in which even the word "tropical" had negative connotations, connecting the Caribbean and South America to Africa) to the present pan-Latin salsa. Today, everyone is invited to the Latin dance party. While tango clubs thrive in Japan, Puerto Rican bomba y plena dances spring up with the spontaneity of mushrooms in New York City's Central Park, entrancing anyone who wants to join the fun. And this vital multicultural and intergenerational exchange seems the most likely trend of the future, as the Americas (North and South) continue to proclaim themselves on the social dance floor.

Latin dances are extremely versatile and mutable; they can fit in anytime and anywhere, bridging between European and non-European dance styles. This mutability may have something to do with the unique position of Latin dance itself, that is neither quite as distal from European as, say, African dances, nor yet quite European in the same way as are social dances like a waltz or fox-trot. Perhaps this is why Latin dances are the dances of the expatriate immigrant who—whether by force or choice—is fragmented between nostalgia for the "old country" and the opportunities of the new.

This bridging is specifically expressed in both the movements of the dancers and the patterns in the music that accompanies them. With the exception of pivots or other quick turning moves required for tango, Latin dance steps are typically performed flat-footed and with a slight bend in the knees. But in closed hold Latin dance partnering, the upper body carriage is comparable to European ballroom and social dance styles. And while European melodies and song lyrics garnish the soul of Latin music, the rhythmic pulse and improvisational call and response in the playing of all kinds of percussive instruments—led by the drum—recalls African tribal affiliations to those whose ancestors were brought into slavery in the New World.

Latin dance occupies a fascinating middle ground as something between the "sweet and the hot," a complex mix of elegant self-control with a little naughty spice slipping out now and then. Latin dances that made it to "the big time" in the United States had packed their bags and moved from rural folk to urban nationalism in South

American and Caribbean cities before arriving. And it was primarily in port cities where these dances flourished and changed: Havana, Cuba, New York City, Miami, Florida, New Orleans, Louisiana, and Buenos Aires, Argentina, where people of all classes, economic status, professions, and cultures mixed, matched, melded, and danced together.

Latin dance suggests an escape, or holiday from the workaday city life of the average American who has grown up under a strong Puritan work ethic. Being on vacation gives people permission to indulge in "non-productive" activities like dancing, something tourists from the United States took full advantage of as they took a short hop across the water from Florida to pre-Castro Cuba in the 1920s to 1930s. This tourist trade brought Cuban dance and music to the forefront, as Havana's hotels and nightclubs rushed to provide the "cigars and rum" that were in short supply back home during Prohibition.

The origin of this dancing "south of the border" tinged with African roots provides a release of inhibitions in controlled and selective venues outside the ordinary life of most Euro-Americans. And while purists and moralists brought Latin dancing under some of the most virulent attacks that any social dancing had been subjected to, far more dancers were of like mind to one Mrs. Lillian Albers who, when faced with the choice between tango or church choir, promptly resigned from the church.[3]

An arbitrary distinction divides Latin dances into two categories; those with the distinctive "Latin motion" of the hips, and those without. Spanish Latin dances are defined as those most directly Spanish, with North African connections like the Argentine tango and its Brazilian cousin the maxixie, bolero (Spanish Cuban), and paso doble (Spain and Mexico). In these, dancer's bodies do not break between the hip and torso, so the line is more closely-connected to other European dances. If there is any Latin motion, it is subtle. Furthermore, the Spanish Latin dances express a different relationship between partners in that the male is dominant. It is his job to show off the lady, just as it is hers to be seen. These Spanish Latin dances are described in Chapter 1, along with other social dances indigenous to the United States under the Latin "influence," such as Conjunto/tejana (Southwestern United States), and Creole zydeco and Cajun (Louisiana and East Texas).

The larger collection of tropical Latin dances has the distinctive Latin motion (also called Cuban motion) of the hips and pelvis, characteristic of Afro-Caribbean dances derived from a combination of African slave dancing and music with European melodies. While the Spanish Latin man shows off his partner, the tropical Latin male dancer has a more inter-cooperative role, expressed in shines, turns, and swings. And in many of these dances, partners take turns in displays of virtuoso improvisation.

These tropical Latin dances are the focus of Chapter 2, in which Cuba leads the way with casino rueda, and tourist versions of the cha-cha, mambo, conga and rumba (also spelled "rhumba"). Columbia's cumbia and Brazil's samba round out the list. The tropical Latin dances incorporate the expressive vertical line "break" of dancers' bodies to a syncopated rolling/swaying of the hips accomplished especially by the female partner in high heels. It is achieved by bending and straightening knees to fit the beat and, along with close body contact between partners, which outraged moral purists. But under that basic concern over morality in dancing couples—and more pointedly as criticism was directed against the female partner—lies the hidden agenda of racism.

Chapter 3 undertakes an investigation of how Latin dances came into the United States. The transition from folk dances of the rural countryside to nationalism in cities like Havana or Buenos Aires caused some of the dances to split between tourist trade versions that were easy to learn and African-based dances that had a much harder time gaining popular mainstream acceptance. The difference between mambo in ballroom instruction studios and mambo at the Palladium in New York City are as night is to day, while rumba brava is a distinct and separate dance in opposition to the notion that any tropical Latin dance is a rumba. Setting the stage for a different approach to Latin social dancing in the United States is the music; from ragtime to jazz. And the complex richness of the tango heritage as it crossed the Atlantic—at least twice—begins to explain how Latin dance supported the Jazz Age and beyond.

The story of what Latin dances did when they got to the United States continues in Chapter 4. The exchanges of the Big Band Era between white, African-American and Latino musicians and dancers bring up social dances tinged with the Latin beat: swing, jive, lindy and jitterbug. As World War II got underway, big band musicians looked for work on Broadway or in Hollywood, or made recordings for sale and radio. Then with the advent of disco and the near-total urban creations of the hustle, lambada, macarena and reggaeton, Latin social dance reinvented itself in late twentieth century style.

Meanwhile, Dominican (bachata and merengue) and Puerto Rican dances (bomba and plena), which had been symbols of nationalism in their own countries, moved into the big cities as part of the Nuyorican cultural identity of Latinos in the United States. In music, this comes out in Latin jazz with the unforgettable songs of Celia Cruz (1925–2003) and mambo-to-Latin jazz great Tito Puente (1923–2000). From the commercialized "new beat jazz" style of Brazil's bossa nova to Latin soul fusions and mixes with other genres, the sound matured. Finally, the eagerly pan-Latin social dance of salsa—indispensible to dance clubs and zumba exercise classes all across the United States—was the result.

Chapter 5 takes another tack altogether, with a more historical view of exchanges between Spanish and tropical Latin exhibition and concert art dance in the United States, from ballet and modern to vaudeville tours. The extremely popular exhibition dance pair of Vernon (1887–1918) and Irene (1893–1969) Castle introduced tango and maxixie to new audiences, first through vaudeville, then in upscale nightclubs and salons, before they created their own dance studio instruction franchises, which further spread Latin social dance and music out from the major cities into every small community of the country.

This trend was accelerated by Latin dances in the movies, performed by the likes of Fred Astaire (1899–1987) and Ginger Rogers (1911–1995). And as Hollywood got caught up in supporting the Good Neighbor Policy, the studios found a lucrative market for stars like the suave Mexican-born Dolores del Rio (1905–1983) and the top-billed "Brazilian bombshell," Carmen Miranda (1909–1955). Hollywood musicians such as Xavier Cugat (1900–1990) and vocalist Desi Arnaz (1917–1986) also frequented television. The exhibition Latin impetus concludes in Chapter 5 with descriptions of present-day capoeira, breaking (or, break dancing), and exhibition wheelchair Latin.

Notes

1. Isabelle Leymarie, *Cuban Fire: the Saga of Salsa and Latin Jazz* (London and New York: Continuum, 2002), 5.

2. Sue Steward, *¡Musica! The Rhythm of Latin America: Salsa, Rumba, Merengue, and More* (San Francisco, CA: Chronicle Books, 1999), 3.

3. Richard M. Stephenson and Joseph Iaccarino, *The Complete Book of Ballroom Dancing* (Garden City, NY: Doubleday & Company, Inc., 1980), 29.

1

Spanish Latin Dances and Others Under the Influence

Attitude is especially heightened in Latin dances. This is no place for the timid, especially for male dancers, whose manner must be confident to the point of domination.

John Reynolds[1]

Dances described in this chapter fall into the general category of Spanish Latin dances. Bolero, paso doble, and the tango are included in ballroom DanceSport competitions, so their position here is pretty well defined. They look a good deal like each other; they don't have the pronounced Latin motion characteristic of tropical Latin dance—if present at all, the motion is subdued. There is a strong connection between them and other social dances that reflect European dance traditions, although non-European dance elements do appear in them.

There are two other distinct dance traditions that fit into this grouping on a slightly different basis. These are dances "under the Latin influence," one might say, of the Spanish Latin form. Although neither one has a fancy pedigree (in fact, they hail from isolated cultures of entrenched poverty and self-sufficiency), Latin motion is not part of their style. Both are homegrown in the United States, and come from strong European dance traditions dating back to before those territories became part of the United States. The song lyrics and culture participating in these dances are non-English: conjunto tejano from the Southwest in Tex-Mex Spanish, and Creole zydeco and Cajun dances from the southwest Louisiana region in French.

Generalizations about Spanish Latin Dances

Exhibition Spanish Latin dances call for fancy dress in dark colors (often black) with bright red accents that at least suggest a Spanish theme. The woman is traditionally costumed in a long, formfitting gown with hair pulled back in a bun, while the man wears a shirt caught at the waist with a cummerbund and trousers, with boots that do not impede his quick footwork. In a bolero routine that shows off its Cuban connection, the dress of the female partner can be short, and her hair may be bobbed. Spanish Latin dancers benefit from some training in ballet technique, as the Spanish folk-classical dances from which these dances take their distinctive style influenced, and were influenced by, ballet's traditional European concert dance technique.

Even amateur Spanish dancers try a ballet-like stance, especially in the carriage of the upper body and arms, which should be clean, curved lines framing the head, and a panther-like "stalking" (predator and prey) line in the walk. This kind of walk is pronounced in the slight turnout of the leg and crossed positions particularly characteristic of the male partner, who with knees in a slight flex, is prepared to move in any defensive or offense position just as if he were fencing. Indeed, the arts of sword and dancing have been historically linked, especially in Spain. So it is understandable that Spanish Latin dances (especially the tango) place partners in torso-protecting positions in relation to one another—that is, offset instead of facing directly front to one another.

Another feature that Spanish Latin dances share with aristocratic European art dance is that the partnered display is something of a fantasy of the masculine point of view; it is a reflection of a social condition in which choreographers, producers, and consumer patrons of the dance were all male. While all Latin dances favor a variety of turns, twists, and shines that shift direction or exchange force and domination between dancers, Spanish Latin dances present the male partner as the overt manipulator, while the female partner's force is presented as covert. By contrast, there is a more egalitarian partnering in tropical Latin dances in which the separation of roles between male and female character is expressed individually.

USA Olympic saber fencers Mariel Zagunis and Becca Ward present tango-like stance. (AP Photo/Andrew Medichini.)

Tango dancers Andrei Udiloff and Christina Zabotto in a partnered lunge. (AP Photo/Dado Galdieri.)

Spanish Latin dances are showy and dramatic. For exhibition and ballroom competition, the lady is swept up into lifts, handed down into floor slides, and supported in deep dips by her partner. But in order to do those kinds of moves, a couple needs a lot of space. For this reason, these dances are only occasionally danced at festivals and private celebration parties, and rarely are they a part of Latin dance club scenes. Some dance studio franchises in the United States offer classes in the Spanish Latin dances, or feature "Latin Dance Nights" so that students of all levels can demonstrate their expertise in preparing for DanceSport competitions.[2] And for the tango, there are groups all over the world offering lessons and opportunities to simply enjoy the complexities of the dance with others in a concentrated—though by no means closed—venue.

Spanish Latin dancers cultivate a "proud" carriage, inherited from aristocratic European roots. Aristocratic court dances across Europe demanded perfection of this disdainful body position that distinguished the aristocracy from ordinary people. And, as a product of the aristocracy, ballet also inherited this dignified carriage. The contributions of Spanish folk dances to this distinction (in flamenco, carriage of the upper body is compared to the strutting of pouter pigeons[3]) is unmistakable.

Bolero

A moderate to slow dance for two, bolero is packed with a depth of romantic seduction. Balancing between Spanish and Cuban cultures, the dance shows its relationship to other Spanish Latin styles with its strong connection to regional folk and classical dances of Spain. At the same time, the dance connects to its New World home in Cuba through a constant percussion rhythm with drums, a feature explored by the classical music composer Maurice Ravel (1875–1937) in his repetitive *Boléro* (1928). The Latin motion of a bolero is subdued into a gently suggestive roll of the lady's hips. Most often danced in the United States as a formal or informal exhibition dance, bolero is sometimes added to American Rhythm competitions. Originating in Spain, the dance is most closely related to the fandango. Phrasing starts with a slow step (side, back, or forward; direct or on a diagonal), making the bolero slow and sensual. This "opening statement" is followed by two quick steps, the last one of which may close next to the other foot (as in a rumba, allowing a small Latin motion for the lady). Otherwise, the third step may extend the line of locomotion across the floor in another direction.

Over time, as the dance caught on in—and adapted its character to—Cuba and the United States, the sound and texture of bolero music heightened its way of communicating elusive and ephemeral emotions that were left too vague for words alone. When bolero peaked in international popularity between the 1940s and 1950s, its music proved attractive to jazz singers, who emphasize its Cuban "feeling."[4]

Bolero not only bridges emotional relationships with quick and slow steps, but also offers a stylistic connection between European and Caribbean culture. Balladic love songs that best suit the dance are in Spanish, yet the Cuban influence is present in soft conga or bongo percussion accents. Like all other Latin dances, bolero can be danced to any popular song that supports its syncopated step pattern, and the inventiveness of partners in interpreting new music for a bolero stretches its identification as such. This quality makes the bolero interesting to perform and to watch.

Stripped of some of the more racy elements of a fandango, bolero has a note of sweet longing to it, so it often makes an appropriate appearance at weddings and anniversary parties. Bolero songs come from the trova, the earliest of patriotic songs steeped in nostalgia and accompanied by the guitar.

In its Spanish version, bolero is usually danced to a 3/4 time, but its Cuban adaptation has dancers in a 2/4 cut, or 4/4 time. Due to the flexibility of bolero's basic step pattern, the dance can transition between variations of sensual desire, starting as a slow and intimate spot rumba with gentle Cuban percussion, then expanding outward into a smooth and fast floor-sweeping charm of a waltz. It is not unusual to find both textures present in a single bolero dance routine, although making these dynamics flow logically from one to the next requires careful coordination between partners. As such, bolero allows some range of "freestyle" expression, but not much improvisation.

The basic hold is close, with full-torso contact between the dancing pair. However, couples often start the dance separated so the introductory walk toward each other may be charged with anticipation and set the mood for the narrative development. As in other Spanish Latin styles, a bolero is clearly directed by the leading male partner, who shows off the lady in turns, holds, dips, and lifts. For her part, the lady exerts her own force with a supple back, graceful arm movements, and leg extensions.

Given its stunning changes of direction, bolero is nevertheless serious and thoughtful. Both the pace and step pattern give this dance its particularly romantic expression. As the dance turns predominantly to the left, the turn is accomplished by a slip pivot, or a way of turning forward or back on the ball of the foot, giving "boléro a very slow, smooth, powerful romantic look and feeling. The boléro is often called the Cuban 'Dance of Love,' because of its slow and dreamy tempo, and its beautiful melodies."[5]

Conjunto Tejano

A faint breeze cools the dry heat of a summer's day as soon as the sun goes down. While heat slowly seeps from rocks and stones, daytime creatures yield the cactus and tumbleweeds to those who prowl the night. A pounding music from accordions, brass-and-reed, and drums spreads out across a dusty air; a single voice rivaling the wail of coyotes laments a love gone wrong, or the injustices endured by the laboring poor. Strings of lights—visible for miles—shine across the patios of homes, restaurants, dance halls, and bars, extending an invitation to all within range to come and dance. The region is the vast open spaces of the American Southwest, where cultural ties to Mexico run strong and the range of the Sonora Desert across political boarders calls to mind a harsh and treeless terrain, rattlesnakes, nail-hard cactus spines, and a sky so blue angels could drown in it. And sharing a desert's disdain for borders, Spanish language and culture in conjunto tejano music and dance spreads in all directions.

Descriptions are also fluid, though they refer to specific identities. The term tejana (feminine) or tejano (masculine) refers to the provinces of Tejas first settled in 1718, part of which later became Texas. Although Texas was first annexed by the United States and then became a state in 1845, the area was contested between Mexico and the United States until Mexico gave up all territory north of the Rio Grande River. The term Norteño refers to all Spanish-speaking people north of that dividing line, including not only Mexican Spanish, but also descendants of original Spanish families who settled the area in the 1600s.[6]

Musically speaking, tejano applies to the entire region of the Southwest, including southern California and Texas. It is from here that música tejano made its way as part of a broad negotiation between

In this March 7, 1995, file photo, Tejano music star Selena poses in Corpus Christi, Texas. (AP Photo/Paul Howell, *Houston Chronicle*, file.)

the Spanish-speaking minority and the dominant English-speaking Americano culture of which it has become a part. The tejano dance music tradition of conjunto also spread into Nebraska and Illinois in 1948, when professional bands began performing in commercial venues.

The term conjunto is more difficult to grasp. The "family" of United States-Mexico border music and the basic dances performed to them are examples of conjunto. The word literally means "put together," and the music is just that: musical instruments, song lyrics, rhythmic pulses, and interrelated styles brought together into a distinctively unified sound as performed by a group of singers and musicians who play together on a regular basis (whether amateur or professional), also called an orquesta tejana.

Originally, the foundational musical instruments of an orquesta tejana were the button accordion (which is also a staple of zydeco and Cajun music), introduced in 1860, and the Mexican twelve-string guitar, called a bajo sexto. The relationship between these instruments was changed by the innovations of Narcisco Martínez (1911–1992, usually referred to as "the father of the modern conjunto"), who "emphasized the right-side melody and treble notes of the accordion, leaving the left-side bass notes to the bajo sexto player."[7] But as orquesta tejana groups moved into mass market recording, the flexibility of conjunto also moved in several, continually intersecting directions at the same time. Corrido remained traditional and immune to mass marketing, despite a little outside experimentation by musicians from other kinds of music. Otherwise, it has largely remained the dance music of agricultural laborers, "at its core a working-class dance music—no matter where it migrated: to California, to the Midwest, and to interior Mexican states."[8]

In the mid-frame, a distinctly Mexican-folk sound from ranchero conjunto became popular through exchanges with country and western as well as rock and roll, so that dancers favoring those music styles could also enjoy a Latin kick on the dance floor. And at the other end of the spectrum, some conjunto groups responded to the 1940s Big Band Era by forming a new sound with horns and saxophones added to guitars and drums, called jaitón (high-toned). This music filled ballrooms for fox-trots, swing dances, and boleros, which were popular with a growing urban Mexican middle-class population. And not just a few Anglos caught up in the Latin dance craze of the movies gave it a try, too.

Conjunto has a distinctive style that makes it unmistakable as soon as it hits the ears, particularly the repeating triplet, melodically and rhythmically accented in the music and expressed by the dancers with a basic step-rock-back-step in a cut time. Couples dancing to this music continuously cross the floor space in close, full-body holds, opening up only to perform a variety of turns. Feet stay close to the floor, and knees are relaxed. There may be a little sway of the hips for the lady, but for the most part, dancers glide smoothly from one space to another, and only a slight lean from one side to another marks a change of musical sequence or a shift of direction. In one dance variation, couples move with a slow and dignified path across the dance floor in "a deliberate, swaying glide reminiscent of a pregnant possum."[9]

Like Cajun, conjunto takes its style from European dances like the waltz and contra dance, and its syncopations from other, non-European sources. The same pattern is also typical of a related dance, cumbia. Like Tejano dances, cumbia has a constantly repeating triplet, and a polka is always lurking somewhere under the steps. But there are some differences; cumbia is faster-paced than Tejano, with long sequences of cascading turns and holds performed in rapid succession.[10] Its lighter, almost skipping pace—suitable to young dancers—has helped cumbia become a staple of quinceañera ("sweet fifteen") celebrations.

Conjunto spread as recording companies took up residence throughout the Southwest starting in the 1920s, and it peaked in production and sales between the 1940s and 1970s. After that, conjuntos split into different directives; while one type settled into something of a "classical" mode, a progressive conjunto movement melded into, and altered, nearby kinds of music. The flexibility of música tejano also made its mark on country and zydeco, further extending the deepest roots of music original to the United States.[11]

So far, the fluid and adaptable nature of conjunto continues to move in new directions. Almost any instrument can be (and probably has been) incorporated into the style. For example, the term "turbo conjunto" of the 1980s expresses this style so clearly that, no matter how it changes, it remains the same. A big, bold sound facilitated the move out of the barrios and into the broader urban dance scene as part of the Latin dance and music revival of the 1990s. Intense experimentation and "flash fads" were—and continue to be—a part of this creative burst, as many a young bilingual Latino musician tries to "make contemporary music without burying [his] native rhythms."[12]

A subgenre of conjunto called banda, for example, is a gunfire-fast paced dance music featuring an insistently blatting tuba, an unlikely musical instrument that serves as a drum or bass beat. Even the farsa (a combination of "frantic" with comic "farce") organ was briefly popular when it was used to meld a synchronized Latin beat with contemporary sounds. No wonder conjunto was cited as an unlikely influence on American psychedelic music in the mid-to-late 1960s. And the current ska fad that started in the late 1990s presents a fusion between "rock en Español" and Southern California skateboard punk, which has washed back into Mexico and Argentina via Jamaica.[13]

Probably an important ingredient of this elasticity with cohesion is language—Spanish and English-Spanish, which is left up to tejano singers to choose as their expressive needs may dictate. The strength of the Norteño songs of Lydia Mendoza (1916–2007), who was titled "la cancionera de los pobres," or "the singer of the poor" kept the conjunto narrative well connected to the cadences of the Spanish language and a soulful recollection of the harsh injustices of poverty. A more recent example is the international stardom of Mexican singer Selena Quintanilla-Pérez (1971–1995), whose popularity as the "Queen of Tejano music" entices even non-Latin dancers out onto the dance floor.[14]

Creole Zydeco and Cajun Dance

They are "the hot and the sweet," two closely-related dance and music styles that are—like conjunto tenjano—pre-national, homegrown traditions of the United States. Separation from mainstream North American mass media and urban culture gave zydeco and Cajun dance music a chance to develop in small house parties and local dance halls of the western regions of Southern Louisiana and East Texas. Firmly grounded in the French language, which colors the

In this April 27, 2008, file photo, Michael Doucet of BeauSoleil performs during the 2008 New Orleans Jazz & Heritage Festival in New Orleans. BeauSoleil, the Grammy-winning Cajun band from Lafayette, recorded its 29th album, which will be released January 20, 2009. (AP Photo/Dave Martin, file.)

tempo, tone, and emotional nuances of the songs, Creole zydeco and Cajun have survived under a dominant, urban and English-speaking population into the millennium, and now they have emerged to claim their space on the contemporary social dance scene.

Zydeco and Cajun are not usually counted among Latin dances, but there is a connection. Deeply rooted in a community tradition of African, European, and Amerindian influences, these dances also reach out into modern-day relevance with a joyful vitality. Cajun couples reflect old-time European contra dance steps and figures as they glide smoothly together across the floor in a calm, dignified upper body stance that any Spanish Latin dancer could admire, and there is no Latin motion. Zydeco's basic step pattern (step-side, together, step-side, touch—or simply a march-like step-touch) is performed with a bent-knee hitch sometimes described as a limp. Dancers in pairs, lines, or mob accent the off-beat with a step and the on-beat with a bend, which breaks the straight vertical line of the body just as Latin motion does in tropical Latin dances. So in zydeco dancing there is a kind of tension between the movements of the dancers and the flow of the music, a directly African response to musical syncopation common in other, more recognizably Latin dances. Also in an Afro-Caribbean vein, zydeco musicians (to the shouts of dancers, observers, and the improvising singers) dance, too—bending backward to the floor, twisting, jumping, or swaying without missing a single stroke of the frottoir or a note on the accordion.[15]

A clear separation of terms describing these dances and their music is first in order. Creole (black) and Cajun (white) are not the same dance music under the name "zydeco," even though they are often conflated in the broader public scene. For the most part, contemporary zydeco events all over the United States include both kinds of dance music as the "sweet (Cajun) and the hot (Creole)." Cajun musicians commonly play zydeco, and Creole musicians include Cajun dance music in their sets. But while outsiders think of these deep-South cultures as mixed up together in a swamp (and there is a substyle from the region called "swamp-pop"), most of the area includes flat land prairies run with cattle instead of alligators. There is a strong cowboy element, especially to Creole music, and the cowboy phrase, "Yippy ti yai ai," may actually have originated from a recurring Creole song theme about a couple of thieving dogs named "Hip et Taiau."[16]

Aside from gas, oil, some fishing, and crops, the region has, throughout the twentieth century, been left alone. Cajun and Creole communities both, regardless of skin color, have always prided themselves on rugged independence and self-sufficiency in an isolated frame. And that has traditionally meant separate. Even in the late 1990s, some non-tourist Cajun dances have been threatened with violence when black musicians have been invited to sit in.[17]

Historically, Cajun refers to the roughly 6,000 French Canadians (Arcadians) who, along with their descendants, left Nova Scotia when the English took over the Acadian peninsula of French Canada in 1755. While some were returned to France, ended up in Haiti, or settled around the East coast of the United States, Arcadians as a cohesive group began making their homes in Southwestern Louisiana around 1760. They were not wealthy. While a very few owned slaves; most worked in the fields alongside of them.

The French lyrics and melodies of Cajun music have a plaintive sadness to them, especially when played on the fiddle. Famed country singer Hank Williams (1923–1953) found the inspiration for his "lonesome" voice in old-time Cajun songs that "dragged" their minor keys. And by way of exchange, contemporary Cajun leans toward the Texas sound in country music. Traditional Cajun dances are slow, sweetly romantic, and dignified, with a very still, upright glide across the dance floor in a basic closed hold. Couples generally danced a two-step, a landler-like waltz (that does not spin round the room, nor do pairs do much turning) and jig, although in the early years other dances like polkas and mazurkas were included.

Most Cajun music is carried by voice, fiddle, keyboard accordion, and pedal steel guitar, with bass, drums, and triangle for the "fais do-dos," or early house dances.[18]

Creole musicians favor a bigger sound to carry the faster "hot" punchy flavor that gets dancers up on their feet for a surprisingly intense zydeco workout on the dance floor. Colorful song phrases are peppered with shouts and wails to the accompaniment of solo saxophone, horns, button accordion, guitar, drums, and washboard (adapted to be worn by the player as a "frottoir").

The term "Creole" is more confusing in its multiple and contradictory uses, "a highly controversial word in south Louisiana, involving a complex, biased web of racial and socioeconomic identities."[19] Academically, "Creole" means anyone with old-world ancestry born

Karl Volkmar and Ann Cross, both of Lafayette, show off their two-stepping at the Festivals Acadiens in Lafayette, La., Saturday, September 17, 2005. (AP Photo/ Rogelio Solis.)

in the Americas, a reference that holds in the Caribbean, "offering one example of south Louisiana's status as the northern frontier of Caribbean culture."[20]

But over time, Creole also applied to light-skinned former slaves who spoke French, those who escaped Haiti after the 1791 revolution, and still others both black and white who, from 1790 to 1803, fled revolution in the Dominican Republic. Individual music traditions and cultural practices between these African-based groups were added to by distinctively Amerindian and French aristocracy cultures. And even between French-speaking and English-speaking former slaves and their descendants living in this area, there are distinctions and disagreements.[21]

Still, dance and music have a way of leaping racist barriers, and no one can deny that there has been—and continues to be—an exchange between Creole and Cajun across common issues. Both grew up in local, self-contained dance parties in the 1940s and 1950s following World War II. And comparable threats to the continuation of their traditions caused them to nearly die out in the 1960s because they were thought of as "old-folks" types of dancing that couldn't compete with the faster-paced and louder music coming out of the radio, television, and the movie theaters.

The move toward an English-only public educational system from 1910 to 1930 (although interviews with old-timers indicate that teachers still punished students for speaking in French or Spanish well into the 1960s[22]) denigrated French-speaking Creole and Cajun songs—like Spanish Norteño song music—as backwater, quaint, and irrelevant. That is, until the late 1970s saw a surge of ethnic pride in the younger generation of musicians eager to reconnect to their roots, and a willingness of the recording industry to market their success to the wider mainstream public.

Zydeco is a product of French-speaking descendants of African-American slaves and former slaves, as well as French-speaking Haitians, but it didn't become known by that term until later. The dance pace is faster than Cajun, and couples perform quick alterations between open and closed holds, making it look something like a jitterbug. Zydeco also encourages large group line dances. The word "zydeco" is often explained as an elision of the French phrase that sometimes appears in song lyrics: "les haricots sont pas salé." Literally translated, "the snap beans are not salty." It is also a metaphor for times so hard that people cannot afford salt pork to season their food. The pronunciation of "les haricots" comes out something like "ze'arco," which is plausible to make up something that sounds like "zydeco."[23]

But the term has had other meanings besides the type of music, including the place to go, the dancing, and the steps of the dance, and—according to old-time fiddler Canray Fontenot—the term "zydeco" wasn't even applied to the music (which was called "la-la") at all. Instead, the word "zydeco" was used as something of a codeword by which only certain guests (who were sure to bring some girls with them) could be invited to "a zydeco" in the limited dance space of a private home.[24]

There are so many important musical groups of this rich heritage that it would be impossible to name them all. Probably the musician of primary credit for styling zydeco into what it is today was Clifton Chenier (1925–1987), who won a Grammy in 1984, and his brother Cleveland, who got the washboard up on the shoulders of the player so the musician could move. Other giants of zydeco are Stanley "Buckwheat" Dural and Queen Ida (first woman to lead a Zydeco band, and 1982 Grammy winner). Old-style and traditional Zydeco musicians include Armadie "tite negre" Adroine and "Rockin' Dopsie," among others. Zydeco stars such as Rosie Ledet, Beau Jocque, and Terrence Simien meld Zydeco styling with other, more urban sound styles like rock and roll, funk, gospel, R & B, and reggae.[25]

Cajun music was recorded in the 1930s and thus preserved; among groups that played into the larger public of the United States was the Hackberry Ramblers, who featured country music in French and English. Progressive Cajun is the trademark of BeauSoleil, started up by Michael Doucet. Popularization of Cajun fiddling was also promoted in mainstream U.S. culture by Doug Kershaw, who performed in several movies such as the 1971 "electronica" Western pop film, *Zachariah*.

Paso Doble

This elegant Spanish-style Latin dance is occasionally included in International Standard Latin Dance ballroom competitions. It also makes a dramatic exhibition dance, though it rarely is performed— due to its usually complex choreography—in casual venues like dance clubs or private parties. Sometimes dance studios feature a paso doble in a "Latin dance night" so that both professional and amateur ballroom dance competitors can rehearse it in front of an audience before facing the judges.

The name paso doble literally means, "two-step," although the dance is also referred to as "the Spanish one-step" with a 2/4-time signature. At its most basic, it is a marching dance to a strong 4/4 time in moderate tempo with most forward steps in the competition form of the dance taken heel first.[26] But over the course of the dance, paso doble partners do just about everything with each other above a simple march.

Showy and dramatic, paso doble tells the story of a ritualistic bullfight in which the man (often dressed in black) displays his red-dressed partner like a matador displays his cape. The two dancers pit themselves together to defeat the raw power of an imaginary bull. The usual music for it is based on that played for bullfights as the matador makes his grand entrance (paseo), or during pauses in the fight when he bows to the cheering crowd. To emphasize the dance as a stylized bullfight, the male partner carries his shoulders down and back, while the head is held high and his line of sight is about where it should be to watch the bull. The high carriage of the torso, pressed-down shoulders, head held high, and sweeping arm gestures are shared by his partner as she is swirled around his body and draped colorfully against his shoulder.

As in a bolero, paso doble partners often begin positioned at separate places on the dance floor before warily moving toward each other. Holds are profoundly close to wide open; lifts, turns, and dips are performed with dramatic phrasing between fast and slow, making paso doble an excellent exhibition dance. Certainly, this is not a dance open to much spontaneous improvisation, and it takes a good deal of practice to effect close coordination. It is also a dance not to be taken lightly:

> In at least its defiant attitude, the paso doble is the equivalent of the tango, with much posturing and little sense of frivolity. During the paso doble, the arms accentuate certain passages in the music, helping to interpret the specialized role of each partner.[27]

Although paso doble presents the drama of a matador and his cape pitted against the bull, the dance actually originated in France, where it became a favorite of the Parisian upper classes during the 1930s. That makes the paso doble a kind of impression of Spanish elegance and exotic passion. The narrative of bullfighter and adversary sometimes played out in a paso doble also suggests a connection with Spanish Mexican folk dances. This is not surprising, as one of the Spanish imports to Mexico is the bullfight, and the deadly "dance"— matador and cape on one side, and the charging passes of the bull on the other—is part of the spectacle. But sometimes there is a change of roles between partners. In some village dances the "Baile del Torito" permits the girl to play the bullfighter as she tries to make her partner fall off the dance platform. Or, the men may wave their handkerchiefs as capes before their partners as if they were the bulls.[28] Paso doble makes a splash wherever it is performed. Recently, ice dancers have tapped the style for exciting exhibition performances, and the 1993 Baz Luhrmann film, *Strictly Ballroom*, concludes its story with a victorious—and somewhat altered—paso doble dance.

Tango and Maxixie

Although the tango is still widely known as "the" quintessential Spanish Latin dance of Argentina, it is closely-related to another dance now rarely seen on the contemporary Latin dance floor. This is the maxixie (variously pronounced "ma SHE she," or "mah she") which, in its heyday of the 1900s to 1920s, was given the notorious title "the original" forbidden dance. Certainly one explanation for the origin of its name, from the prickles of a cactus plant, suggests a dangerous relationship.[29] Another possible origin of the word is a kind of pickle. Also called "tango Brésilien" (or, Brazilian tango), maxixie was originally a Brazilian folk dance. Along with the tango, it was one of the only two Latin dances chosen by the exhibition dance duo, Vernon and Irene Castle, to be refined, tamed, and cleaned up for exhibition ballroom performances and instruction to refined upper-class couples.[30]

Watching a tango and a maxixie dance, most people would have a hard time telling them apart—they have so much in common. Although neither dance shows off much "Latin motion" of the hips to signal an Afro-Hispanic parentage, tangos and maxixies still move dancers through the steps and figures with a bent-knee recognition of gravity typical of Spanish Latin dances. Although tame in sexual innuendos, by modern standards, both dances were once considered scandalous, setting off the alarms of social degradation among moralists because they featured an extremely close, full-body offset hold between partners, in which the dancers' legs entwine.

To make matters even more shocking, the man steps backward not in "retreat," but in order to lean back and draw his partner even more closely over his body, "a vertical expression of a horizontal desire," as one description puts it.[31] While upper-class men could generally tango the night away in any way they liked without anyone so much as raising an eyebrow, public outrage was directed at wealthy women who, around 1914, regularly attended afternoon "tango teas" while their husbands worked. Although the professional male dancers at

tango teas were looked down upon, they gave the ladies a thrill of risk and danger; and sometimes a little more:

> The main concerns of nearly all the anti-tango salvos launched by individual clergy were the degradation of women, the immodest and immoral behavior of women who danced, and the effect on home and society when women lost their sense of decency and propriety. Rarely is a word directed toward men who danced.[32]

Certainly, tangos and maxixies were easy to weave together into one steamy compulsion driven by the man whose complete concentration of the moment was on his female partner; at least, that's how early Hollywood presented it. It is a matter of question whether or not the "tango" performed in silent films such as *Blood and Sand* (1922) or *Four Horsemen of the Apocalypse* (1921) really was a tango, a maxixie, or an apache (a Paris underworld street dance that attracted tourists with its violence). Quite likely the Italian-American who turned into the "Latin lover" (and sometimes Arab sheik), Rudolf Valentino (1895–1926), put into his dances a combination of all three as he saw fit to apply them to "mesmerize" the female object of his interest.

The maxixie underwent a number of complicated transformations before taking its modern form. The original maxixie is essentially a combination of a versatile couples' version of the Brazilian batuque with a fandango. Until the samba overtook it, this hybrid was the most popular dance of Brazil. Late in the 1700s, it was called the lundú, and was danced by all classes of Brazilians. In the mid-1800's, Portuguese, Spanish, and French immigrants introduced the polka, which was quickly taken up by lundú dancers and given the new name of "polka lundú." It was danced something like a samba, because the partners leaned away from the direction in which they were going. And it was considered vulgar. So the maxixie was something of a Brazilian polka or two-step that wasn't welcome in fine society, but which was danced with abandon for exhaustingly long periods of time by the lower classes. But the dance also caught on outside of Brazil because it fit very well with ragtime rhythms in the United States and Europe.[33]

Tango is the premier Spanish Latin dance designated as the national dance of Argentina, although it is important to mention that the other country and city across the Rio de la Plata from Buenos Aires— Montevideo, Uruguay—also contributed to its richly complex expression.[34] The precise origins of this infamous dance are unknown, and even a definitive description of a tango is not possible:

> One has only to observe that 36 books and articles devoted to the tango are listed as bibliography under the Grove's Musical Dictionary "tango" entry to see the point. Its origins never completely defined, the tango remains a mystery, a myth—a dance "remembered" even by those who have never seen it.[35]

Is the tango just a dance pulled up out of the seamy criminal underworld of Buenos Aires and tamed into respectability? Even the name of the dance is shadowy. Does the word "tango" come from the Latin word tangre (meaning to touch), or might the name come from a North African dance called a tangano, suggesting rhythmic drums or an ancient flamenco dance? The older versions of tango had the taint of the low-class and criminal element to them; the tango meant not only a style of dance, but also a certain kind of gathering of dance and music:

> In 1830, tango meant something entirely different from what the word means today. It was not a specific dance at all, but rather, an event (as in, an "all-night tango") involving any kind of dancing that black people did to drums.[36]

The name of the dance is only the beginning of tango's ambiguity. Closely related on the Spanish side of its heritage is flamenco. But flamenco is itself of mixed origins. Brought into Spain by the Rom, flamenco reflects the accumulation of many different cultures overlaid with a sense of loss and longing held deep in the heart of the exile. The Rom, who probably left the northwest regions of India (not, as their common name of "Gypsies" might suggest, from Egypt), spread across Europe over centuries to settle in the South of Spain, birthplace of flamenco.[37] There, their dancing was enriched with Moroccan dances; after all, it is a very short distance between Spain and Morocco across the Straight of Gibraltar.

A tango is a tango is a tango—or is it? Although more writing has been done on this Latin dance than nearly any other, no two descriptions quite agree. Otherwise, details are fluid. Still, the tango has permeated popular culture and media in the United States, as the intense posing of a tango lends itself to many comic parodies of mock seriousness, particularly when flatly paced off by a cheek-to-cheek pair clutching each other to the Billy Vaughn tune, *Hernando's Hideaway*, with roses clutched in their teeth. A more serious tango tune that has become ubiquitous is the 1935 *Por una Cabeza* (music by Carlos Gardel and lyrics by Alfredo Le Pera), which has been featured in no less than thirteen movie and television show tango scenes.

Tango is extremely adaptable. It can move a pair across a large ballroom floor, or confine itself, as can flamenco, to the approximate space of a tabletop in a crowded dance hall. Out in the street, along the boulevards, or even onboard a ship, tango fits itself into every kind of space. It has even provided enticing choreography for ice dancing. Variation in the skills of the dancers can be accommodated; at least two Hollywood movies (*Scent of a Woman*: 1992 and *Flawless*: 1999) feature disabled men leading their partners in tango. While novice dancers can quickly learn the basic steps, an experienced pair of tangoistas can manage an astonishing array of complex rapid kicks, toe-heel placements, changes of direction, twists, and pass-throughs; all without losing upper body contact.

There are several major—and many minor—styles of tango danced worldwide; of these, the Argentine, Continental, and English have various positions, characteristic closed holds, and steps. Argentine-style has a closed hold between partners that is slightly different than others, and devotees claim is as the only "true and authentic" version. Modern tango has taken on a more aggressively masculine look than earlier versions, as the male partner dominates and the female winds herself around his show of strength.

Originally, the tango was danced in a 2/4 time; currently it is in 4/4 (slow, slow, quick, quick, slow). The older milonga tango with a habanera accompaniment had more in common with Cuban folk dance, emphasizing leg movements, full-body contact, foot shuffling, a gripping cheek-to-cheek embrace, and quebrada (swiveling of the hips). This sliding "shuffle" and low center of gravity further marks the tango as a dance influenced by older, strongly African dances.[38]

Drama in the dance comes from combinations of extremely fast movements with slow, drawn-out pauses and poses. In terms of locomotion, steps the dancers take in any direction make the most out of a hesitation; a kind of lingering of the finishing step to the last possible instant needed to take the next step. Sharpness is achieved by a "drag" in the rhythmic response of the non-supporting foot. In other words, the tango dancer delays until the last possible instant in placing weight upon it, making the shift of weight very suddenly.

The effect of this dragging hesitation suggests conflicting emotions in the dance. The foot lingers in the last count as if reluctant to leave a sweet memory, then in a quickly aggressive shift, the dancer signals an eagerness to meet the next count. Other quick movements such as sudden turns, feet that dive in and round each other, and knee-snaps like the flash of daggers, contrast with languorous dips and leans. There are a few climactic moments (in a more modern tango that isn't "regulation ballroom style," that is) in which the dancing pair face full-front to one another, as if sharing a brief instant of clarity and union; otherwise, quick head-snaps away from one another are the rule as partners avoid direct eye contact and instead face the direction in which they are moving together. For the man:

> Feet are usually closed after a step to the side. [But for the woman] in heels, a faint lead by the inside edge of the ball of the foot meeting the floor first, or with the left heel near the right instep emphasizes the curves of her body and gives a distinctly feminine sculptural quality to her pause.[39]

For both partners, pose in tango is everything—its moments of stillness as potent of strength and force as its most lighting-quick footwork. Despite its suddenly rapid moves, a tango is a dance of leisure, of walking; the tango owes its unique style to the way in which the feet are placed on the ground. "All walking steps in the tango are [as in the art of fencing] picked up from the floor slightly and placed into position."[40] There is no "rise" or body sway in a tango. Shoulders are level and knees are kept in a slight flex to accommodate quick changes of direction. The lady moves more to the right side of the man, in a classically-ordained gender position; possibly originating in Western culture long before the ancient Egyptians, in which the woman stands to the right of the man as was canonically standardized in classical Greek and Roman art.

Eventually, a European version and an American version of the tango settled sometime between 1911 and 1925 to fit tango steps into eight general categories:

> Corté (cut; almost like a polka—includes a stop during which both partners suddenly stop for two beats, then resume moving)

La Marcha (the march)

Grapevine (step side-step behind-step side-step front)

Paseo (passing)

Ochos (figure eights)

Ruedas (circles)

Media Luna (half-moon, or fan step; the foot describes a wide arc to the left)

Molinette (windmill)

Both the International Standard ballroom and American Smooth DanceSport competitions include the tango. It is "the only Standard or Smooth dance without an Anglo-Saxon heritage"[41] perhaps due to its European roots in classical Spanish tradition and absence of Latin motion. Competition tango was the last of the Standard ballroom dances added in 1931. Danced to a 2/4 time at a tempo of about 33 bars per minute, this form of tango has a staccato style characteristic of moving in the flat plane and sharp moves introduced by dancers Freddie Camp and Alida Pasqual in 1935. "Camp had the ability to accelerate explosively from stillness to vigorous action, then to reassume a static posture pregnant with expectation of the next movement."[42]

Perfectly prim and proper in its competition form—the hold is close but not quite in full-torso contact—tango can be pleasing and formal, if a little cold. Partners take a "promenade" position, which is like a waltz hold except that the lady's left hand is held in a "cut" position across the gentleman's right shoulder blade, or she may hold the back of her partner's upper right arm.[43]

This form of tango retains a little of its old disreputable allure in the close-embrace style of the dance, in which the dancers constantly maintain upper body contact. The close embrace does not permit much fancy footwork, and there would be no room for it anyway on a crowded dance floor.[44] The elegant carriage of the upper body floats above rapid foot and leg actions of twists, turns, kicks, and dips close to the center of gravity of the dancers. In moving across the floor, the tango gentleman's left foot strides forward in a "military" advance, forcing the lady backward into a retreat or defense position. The attitude is serious; couples hold strict to form, and there is little or no emotion involved. "All joy is abandoned in the tango. This is a serious pastime practiced by those with little to gain and nothing to lose—especially innocence and trust."[45]

A pair of street tangoistas in full body contact. (AP Photo/Anne Ryan.)

Rich with clean, sleek moves, quick changes in direction, and iconic poses, tango never ceases to intrigue its audiences or appeal to its dancers, whether professional or amateur. Above all, the tango is a serious and intense dance of complex relationships and fired emotions kept strictly—if barely—in check; an exchange of intimacy and isolation; trust and betrayal; love and hate. And all of it passes back and forth between the exclusive connections—and disconnections—of a pair in dance.

Notes

1. John Lawrence Reynolds, *Ballroom Dancing: The Romance, Rhythm and Style* (San Diego, CA: Laurel Glen Publishing, 1998), 40.

2. Author's unpublished notes as research assistant to Florida State University professor Dr. Carolyn Picart (July, 2001).

3. Author's unpublished journal notes (Granada, Spain, January 4, 1969).

4. Sue Steward, ¡Musica! The Rhythm of Latin America: Salsa, Rumba, Merengue, and More (San Francisco, CA: Chronicle Books, 1999), 42–43.

5. http://www.dancelovers.com (accessed: May 10, 2010).

6. Manuel Peña, "Música Tejana: The Music of Mexican Texas," In Robert Santelli, Holly George-Warren, and Jim Brown, Eds. American Roots Music (New York: Harry N. Abrams, 2001), 126–143.

7. Teresa Palomo Acosta, Handbook of Texas Online http://www.tshaonline.org/handbook/online/articles/MM/fmadk.html (accessed: May 11, 2010).

8. Peña, 130.

9. Peña, 132.

10. Youtube: cumbia leyana and tejano (accessed: May 5, 2010).

11. Peña, 140.

12. Ed Morales, The Latin Beat: The Rhythms and Roots of Latin Music from Bossa Nova to Salsa and Beyond (Cambridge, MA: Da Capro Press, 2003), Introduction: xxiv.

13. Morales, Introduction: xxi.

14. Rick Mitchell, "Selena," In Houston Chronicle, online May 21, 1995 (accessed: May 30, 2010).

15. Ben Sandmel and Rick Olivier, Zydeco! (Jackson, MS: University Press of Mississippi, 1999), 12.

16. Ann Allen Savoy, "Cajun and Zydeco: The Musics of French Southwest Louisiana," In Robert Santelli, Holly George-Warren, and Jim Brown, Eds. American Roots Music (New York: Harry N. Abrams, 2001), 83.

17. Sandmel, 75.

18. Savoy, 109.

19. Sandmel, 16.

20. Sandmel, 15.

21. Savoy, 109.

22. Author's unpublished journal notes, Taos, NM: 1972–1973.

23. Sandmel, Savoy, et al.

24. Sandmel, 41.

25. www.frenchcreoles.com/MusicEvents/Zydeco (accessed: April 23, 2010).

26. http://www.dancehistory.hit.bg/l_paso_doble_en.html (accessed: May 13, 2010).

27. John Lawrence Reynolds, Ballroom Dancing: The Romance, Rhythm and Style (San Diego, CA: Laurel Glen Publishing, 1998), 43–44.

28. Francis Toor, A Treasury of Mexican Folkways (New York: Crown Publishers, Inc., 1979), 368–369.

29. Sonny Watson's Streetswing.com Archives streetswing.com/histmain/d5index (accessed: August 8, 2009).

30. Don McDonagh, "Twentieth-Century Social Dance before 1960," In Selma Jeanne Cohen, Ed. International Encyclopedia of Dance, Vol. 5 (New York: Oxford University Press, 1999), 626–631.

31. Micol Seigel, "The Disappearing Dance: Maxixe's Imperial Erasure," In Black Music Research Journal 25, no. 1–2 (2005), questia.com/PM.qst?a=o&d=5020426011 (accessed: April 17, 2010).

32. Jo Baim, Tango: Creation of a Cultural Icon (Bloomington and Indianapolis, IN: Indiana University Press, 2007), 7.

33. Baim, 50.

34. John Charles Chasteen, *National Rhythms, African Roots: The Deep History of Latin American Popular Dance* (Albuquerque, NM: University of New Mexico Press, 2004), 102.

35. Anna Kisselgoff, "The Tango Whirls with Passion," *The New York Times* (1923–current file); October 20, 1985; ProQest Historical Newspapers, The New York Times (1851–2006) H18.

36. Chasteen, 6.

37. *Latcho Drom* (safe journey) a documentary on the history of the Rom (directed and written by Tony Gatlif, 1993).

38. Chasteen, 19.

39. Moore, 227.

40. Moore, 224.

41. Reynolds, 59.

42. Yvonne Marceau, "Ballroom Dance Competition," In Selma Jeanne Cohen, Ed. *International Encyclopedia of Dance*, Vol. 1 (New York: Oxford University Press, 1999), 358.

43. Moore, 222.

44. Chasteen, 7.

45. Reynolds, 43.

2

Tropical Latin Dances

Salsa's magic has always been transmitted from skin to skin—in a silent, seductive dance clinch, and through a sheet of dried goat skin—the voice of the drum. To many displaced young Latinos all over the world salsa is a validation—it is home, a flag, and grandma.

Willie Colón[1]

Generalizations about Tropical Latin Dances

Founding salsero Willie Colón refers to the international, pan-Latin social dance known as salsa in the statement above, but his apt comment applies to all tropical Latin dances. Many of them have gone into making salsa what it is today—a topic taken up in greater detail in Chapter 4. So to some degree, by starting out treating these tropical Latin dances as separate kinds of dances—by defining their steps, figures, moods, music, venues, and histories—we lay the groundwork on which a discussion of Latin jazz and salsa can be understood.

To dance is to state who you are, where your roots lie, the community to which you belong. And the way in which couples, individuals, and groups respond to the beat—as simple as whether or not to take a step on the first or second note of the music—announces the nature of those roots, regardless of where and how the many branches of Latin dance may grow. Latin music provides the "closed hold" between tropical Latin dances and the pulses by which they are identified, to the core of identity and meaning.[2] Tropical Latin dances here mean those Latin social dances with ties—whether recognized or not—with African American culture, especially through the syncopated clave five-count beat and the "break" of the vertical line of the dancing body that is generally achieved through hip movements called Latin motion.

The term "tropical" refers to those dances primarily from the Caribbean islands: Puerto Rico, the Dominican Republic, and especially, Cuba. Colombia and Brazil are also included as the styles of their dances are similar. Although tropical Latin dances are clearly distinct from Spanish Latin dances, it is important to remember that vigorous exchanges between them are ongoing. While a few Spanish Latin dances allow a subtle roll of the hips now and then, tropical Latin dances break the line of the dancers' bodies in sharp, often very quickly executed moves. The syncopation of the music and the way that the steps fit the music allow for sways, rolls, and jerks of the dancers' hips in the process of performing the steps. This movement can be part of a locomotive move across the floor, or performed "in place" with a great range of expressive meaning: flirtatious, taunting, seductive, or rejecting. This is a lateral hip movement that "breaks" the body's vertical line, and rhythmically performed from side to side, produces a sinuous, flowing motion of the dancer's torso. For the "breaking hip movement they have many names, usually involving some form of the verb 'break' (quebrar or recquebrar)."[3]

This movement and line of the body is especially emphasized in the female partner wearing heels, an essential feature of her costume even when the rest of her outfit is street casual. The focus of Latin motion on the pelvis and its expressiveness through strategic bending and straightening of the knees come from the strong influences of dances from Africa. These were brought westward across the Atlantic with the slave trade, first to the Caribbean countries. From there, they spread into the United States and South America. Latin motion is also sometimes called Cuban motion, because Cuba (from the Amerindian word "cubanacan," meaning center place), is the island where the distinctive Latin rhythm originated; hence the designation "Afro-Cuban" for the rhythms driving most tropical Latin dances.

That rhythm is fundamentally expressed as the clave, a word with a richly complex series of interrelated meanings. To begin with, "clave" is the Spanish word for "keystone" or "key," and also the clef scale in musical notation. Claves are the indispensable percussion

Young ballroom dance competitors demonstrate Latin motion break in a tropical Latin dance routine. (© Stanislav Pobytov/iStockPhoto.com.)

instrumental accompaniment for tropical Latin dances. They are made of two pieces of carved wood that are struck together for a sharp, bright sound, achieved when each clave is slightly loose in the hand, so the wood can resonate a little.

Like their close relative, castanets, quality wooden claves are "gendered" to present a partnership mirrored in the couples dancing to its beat. The lower-toned "male" clave rests in a loosely-cupped left hand. The striker, or "female" clave, toned at a slightly higher pitch, is held in the right hand to be struck against the "male" (for a left-handed musician the claves are reversed).[4] The composition of the wood of each individual pair of claves determines where their "sweet spots" will provide a rich and resonant sound. Special effects, such as rolls, can be obtained by holding the claves parallel to each other and striking them end to end. "Fernando Oritz, a Cuban musical historian, has said that the claves doubled as 'pegs of hard wood used in the making of ships,' adding another meaning—"clavo" in Spanish means "nail."[5] Anyone able to hold a steady beat can quickly learn to play them (they are often included among instruments for young children to learn rhythm). But this simple instrument produces a complex series of rhythmic patterns, each one of which signals corresponding nuances of movement in couples on the dance floor.

The sound of the claves is a Cuban musical invention synonymous in tourists' imaginations with swaying palm trees, pristine beaches, rum-filled drinks, and leisure. Clave beat is believed to have originated in the eastern province of Cuba called Oriente toward the end of the nineteenth century, where it was played by small—thus highly mobile—bands comprised of six musicians (called sextetos), using guitar or tres, maracas, güiro, claves, bongo, a marimbula, and a botija. The more urban style played in Havana at the beginning of the century became the national music in 1920, displacing danzón. Soneos were the improvised lyrics and melody sung during a montuno, or vocal interlude, while the sonero was the singer skilled at improvising.[6] But no matter where these elements ranged in content or improvisational daring, they were all held together by the five-count clave beat. "According to veteran conga player Joe Cuba, 'Clave makes the (Latin music) world go round.' "[7]

Tropical Latin dance and music also describe oppositions and harmonic combinations of opposites. A "clave rhythm" is the basis of all authentic Tropical Latin music rhythms, creating a signature style of syncopation as distinct from, though closely related to, jazz: " ... whether it's a slow bolero or an out-and-out guaguancó."[8] The repeated five-strike pattern (technically, a cinquillo) can be performed as a "forward clave rhythm" of three notes followed by two (some-times called the "Cuban" or son clave, a 3/2 rhythm), or as a "reversed clave rhythm" of two notes followed by three (a 2/3, rumba, or African pattern). Once the rhythmic pattern is established, it remains constant throughout the piece, providing the basis for musical improvisation by singers and/or musicians.[9]

Seven of these popular and familiar tropical Latin dances are described here; they are all dances of Caribbean and South American origins that have made good in the United States. As such, they have become staples of Latin dancing all across the country, favored not only in formalized style for ballroom and DanceSport, but also as informal dances (past and present) in Latin dance clubs and family celebrations. These dances have contributed to the Latin jazz creation of salsa, which, in a single dance set, may find dancers all over the world in merengues, casino ruedas, bachatas, congas, cumbias, cha-chas, or sambas simultaneously on the same dance floor; a semi-organized riot of fun for anyone brave enough to give it a shot.

Cuba and Puerto Rico (which, according to poet Lola Rodríguez de Tío, are like two wings of the same bird[10]), top the list, with Cuba's casino rueda, cha-cha, conga, and dance studio versions of mambo and rumba (also spelled "rhumba"). Because mambo and rumba both have two very different versions (the alternate spelling of "rhumba" serves as a point of distinction between them), a more complete account of them is taken up in Chapter 3. The predominance of these dances has to do with the relatively early introduction of tourist versions of them into the United States. During Prohibition (also called The Noble Experiment from 1920 to 1933), enterprising U.S. mafia and local Havana businesses recognized a mutual profit in attracting wealthy tourists from the United States to enjoy forbidden pleasures in "the land of rum and cigars."[11] In fairly short order, luxury hotels and exotic nightclubs sprang up in Havana to accommodate this lucrative trade.

To some extent, Puerto Rico also benefitted from the tourist trade. Today, two Puerto Rican dances, bomba and plena, are sometimes interchangeably enjoyed to the same music, and the pair of longtime Dominican Republic dances, the bachata and merengue, have become staples of tropical Latin dancing. Because these Puerto Rican and Dominican dances play an important role in the development of Latin dances in the United States, they are described in greater detail in Chapter 4. Samba from Brazil, and cumbia from Columbia, round out the list.

While Spanish Latin dances emphasize the dramatic seriousness of deeply-felt emotions between couples, tropical Latin dances show off a contrasting, quick-paced flirtation. That doesn't mean these dances can't have their lyrically romantic moments. But they are more likely to provide the "hot chili peppers" on the dance floor favored by the young and athletic, which feature a fairly consistent marathon "step-a-beat" attack. Fast knee-snap kicks, spins, twirls, bends, twists, and dips, and plenty of upper body as well as lower body expressive movements, make these dances something to watch and even more to dance—with or without a partner. A step or touch comes on every beat of the music without the emphasized pause (as if the music is waiting for the dancers to continue) of Spanish Latin forms. Even when tropical Latin dancers aren't moving, the drive of the beat is still implied, and its imperious momentum must be obeyed.

Exhibition tropical Latin dancing is especially entertaining to watch, and media cameras adore the fast, snappy moves, as evidenced by the popularity of cha-cha, samba, and mambo for such TV shows as *Dancing with the Stars* or *So You Think You Can Dance*. Tropical Latin dance costumes, particularly in exhibition and DanceSport versions, are very showy with plenty of skin, especially putting on display the woman's powerful and curvaceous physique. Short skirts, cleavage, midsections of ribcage to belly button dives with plenty of fringe and glitter to emphasize her rapid movements of hips, legs, and arms, and bobbed short hair are usual. Gentlemen may also go in for extreme fashion and colors complimenting those of his partner, with shirts slashed to the waist and tight-fitting trousers.

Yet, there is a kind of egalitarian exchange between partners in these dances that is distinct from Spanish Latin dances; the lady holds her own on somewhat the same level as her gentleman. Equal opportunity exists for virtuoso display; both partners twirl, turn, and swing out away from each other and then come back close together, in that fundamental figure eight pass that brings these dances in dialogue with other popular social dances. In fact, the lady often holds the basic step pattern while her partner takes the stage with improvisational bravado.

Casino Rueda

Sometimes also called a rueda de casino, this charming dance for two or more couples is danced in a "wheel" or circular pattern on the dance floor (like musical chairs), making it a great mixer dance for a party group to get acquainted. The dance does take up a bit of space, depending on the number of couples in the wheel; however, there may be two or more circles, though coordination on which group is moving toward the center of the wheel and which is moving out can get pretty tricky. The wheel, or wheels, turn around the dance floor as couples periodically change partners during the dance—men moving in a counterclockwise direction around the perimeter of the wheel, and women moving clockwise. Everyone keeps track of the center of the wheel, maintaining a circular relationship with everyone else, regardless of partners (which may sometimes be same-sex).

Group class practicing salsa moves based on a variety of popular tropical Latin dances. (© craftvision/iStockPhoto.com.)

Some of the most charmingly interesting features of a rueda are the quick changes between group unison moves and pairs that move both in and out, as well as around, the perimeter of the wheel. As performed on today's dance floors, the dance is often called a "salsa rueda," but can also be a merengue or bachata rueda with steps and music to match. Figures may even include a conga line (in a circle, of course). In addition to swing moves, holds, turns, and dips, the rueda can include claps and jumps and even a quick "Texas star" square dance turn (gents on the inside). In order to keep everyone together, the rueda leader—much as does a bomba leader—uses hand signals to mark changes or call in the figures, a very useful tactic on a crowded and noisy dance floor.

Despite its current popularity in the salsa family of Latin dances in the United States, casino rueda has been around a while, having got its start some time around 1950 in the Havana social club of El Casino Deportivo.[12] The name "casino" probably came from one of the oldest table gambling games (roulette) in which the casino wheel spins clockwise, while the ball rolls counterclockwise before falling into its slot.

Probably the best Broadway/Hollywood dance rueda is found in the beginning of "The Gym Dance" in *West Side Story* (1957 Broadway and 1961 United Artists film) with music by Leonard Bernstein and choreography by Jerome Robbins. While the rueda is meant to mix the girls and boys at random, this one instantly disintegrates along gang lines, pointing out the hatred between Jets and Sharks just before Maria and Tony meet each other. As the dance progresses (amid shouts of "mambo!"), each group tries to outdo the other in athletic dance moves and figures. And there is a whole lot more going on besides mambo; a bit of cha-cha, lindy, jive, ballet, and even a few fandango stomps—just to keep straight who is Puerto Rican and who is Irish.

Cha-Cha

Also called the cha-cha-cha, this is a carefree, cheeky, and flirtatious couples dance with five beats (two of which are "silent" and three for the triple "cha") in a 4/4 bar phrasing. Adaptable and versatile, the syncopated rhythm of cha-cha sets up a playful exchange between partners, who alternate between open and closed holds. This fast-paced tropical Latin dance from Cuba is thought to have been named for the seed pod of the West Indies that was used as a rattle, a pace-setting percussion for both sacred and secular dancing events.[13] Other possible meanings of the word include a chacha (or nursemaid) or chachar (the chewing of cocoa leaves). It also might come from the guaracha, another lively jíbaro dance music style of Spanish/Cuban/ Puerto Rican origins reflected in modern Latin music.

There are various reports on how the cha-cha was discovered and brought into the United States. Officially introduced in 1954, by 1959 it was the most requested dance at the studios. One story has it that in 1952, an English dance teacher named Pierre Lavelle observed a rumba-style dance in some of the dance clubs in Havana, and dubbed it the cha-cha-cha for its distinctive triplet brushing sound at the end of each five-count phrase.

It is also possible that cha-cha refers to the sounds the dancers make with their feet. While traditional voodoo bands used the cha-cha rattle with three drums and a bell to pace the singing and dancing associated with spiritual rituals, the rattle also paced celebratory kinds of social dancing in the urban setting of Havana, where some of the "less inhibited night clubs and dance halls" of Havana featured a "triple mambo." And in fact, the cha-cha is sometimes referred to as an easier form of mambo. The shuffling sound produced by the feet of these triple mambo dancers (assuming the music paused for those beats so the sounds of the feet could be heard) sounded like a rattle.[14]

Dances with a "shuffle" reflect pale shadows of indigenous African dances, remnants of which were brought with slaves to the New World as circle dances. Slave owners were uneasy over any slave gathering for dancing or celebration; after all, in at least two instances of insurrection, the attacks had been preceded by a bout of dancing. Laws prohibiting or restricting the use of drums and gatherings were passed in the early 1800s. But the close connection between dancing and good health did not go unremarked by slavers, and a complete ban on dancing was not possible anyway.

A compromise of sorts was reached. African-based circle dances were changed into "ring shouts," which were not defined as dancing by prohibiting Baptist churches; "as long as the feet or legs did not cross"[15] or there wasn't any jumping involved. Shuffles were substituted as a means of locomotion across the dancing area by slaves to officially comply—and indirectly defy—these restrictions. As a result, shuffles are integral to the technique of various tap dance styles and jazz pioneered in African cultures transplanted to the Americas.

But the cha-cha is not just an import from African culture; it owes much of its intrigue to a dose of European dances, too. Formal dances based on country dances collectively called contradanza arrived in Cuba in the 1700s along with some of Europe's most aristocratic families. This social dance played out for a while, but pretty soon dancers began to tire of the "choreographic stiffness" of contradanza. The syncopated beat in other, less-proper kinds of music and dance brought into Havana by French refugees starting around 1830 encouraged some of the more adventurous contra dancers to improvise, perhaps spurred on by musicians who also altered their style to fit modern tastes:

> In 1953 the Cuban Orchestra América started playing the time-honored danzón with a new syncopated beat. This sounded like a very slow Mambo, and Cuban dancers used a slight triple-hip undulation on the slow count.[16]

This different kind of Cuban dancing (which, as often happens with new dances, caused society censors to quickly brand it as immoral) was called danzón, and it became the foundation of both cha-cha and its close relative, the mambo.[17] These two dances provide a pleasing contrast in couples dancing and went well together. But while the mambo hitched a ride into New York City where it found a home in the vital exchanges between African-American dancers and Cuban musicians, the sweeter nature of a cha-cha became popular in Cuba itself, where tourists picked it up and also brought it into the United States.

The basic cha-cha step is tricky, but well worth the effort to learn; a double-quick alternated with a triple beat (the distinctive cha-cha-cha at the end of the phrase) on a "cut" time makes up the basic step. This allows the dancer a step-ball-change that may or may not alter the direction of locomotion with a Latin movement; the phrasing bridges measures with the triple count landing on counts four and one (something like a "triple lindy"). As a dance-for-two, cha-cha offers an opportunity to display class as well as speed. The shoulders of both partners are kept quiet. In its various open positions such as shines, the arms of both partners in a cha-cha are held out at shoulder level with palms down, a gesture reminiscent of its contradanza origins. For front shines, partners bend toward each other, and shake their shoulders with playful eye-to-eye contact; the gesture evolved into a carioca head-to-head contact made popular by Fred Astaire and Ginger Rogers in their Latin dancing movies.

Back-to-back shines allow for close partner precision of steps and moves, or even mirrored reversals that add intriguing dimensions to the partnership. Finally, the cha-cha "chase" figure allows a parallel shine with the man in front, or the woman in front, moving together in the same direction (not unlike a vaudeville routine, or movie musical number). A tightly-clenched, closed-hold position torso-to-torso in the cha-cha called a "cuddle" is apparently custom-made to curl the hair of any moralist—to the delight of the ever-young and trendy.

Although the cha-cha has many variations designed to show off a sparkling variety of couples' dance moves, it can also feature short bursts of solo sequences. Here the individual dancer expresses his or her response to the music in turn. However, unlike other tropical Latin styles, cha-cha is not amenable to actual improvisation, because close coordination between partners is essential.

Overall, cha-cha is a satisfying spot dance in clubs or other social dance venues where space is limited. And on occasion, it also makes a stunning exhibition dance for couples to "strut their stuff" across the floor. In order to get up the footwork speed, cha-cha students (as with other fast tropical Latin dances) practice close and fast-paced steps while grasping a pole, so that they can accurately aim the tiny steps, kicks, and twists to match those of their partner. This practice technique also builds up speed in the various body isolations demanding a high degree of physical stamina and control for both the gentleman and the lady.

Cha-cha reached its peak of popularity on social dance floors in the United States around 1980, and then faded into the background as something of a "dated" kind of dance that might be mentioned in a campy detective novel. But it is still ideally suited to exhibition dance routines and is featured as one of the more spectacular dances in both Rhythm American and International Latin ballroom DanceSport competitions. And cha-cha also contributes to the current Latin dance scene as part of salsa.

Cumbia

One of the most interesting gifts of Colombia, cumbia dance and music makes a unique union of both Spanish Latin and tropical Latin dance styles to a music enriched by both Amerindian and African rhythms. Originally danced to the accompaniment of flutes, drums, and shakers, the basic form of cumbia probably came from African slave populations along the coast of Colombia as a social courtship dance that originated in Guinea, called cumbé.

But European influences are equally strong: "According to legend, a German shipwreck that washed up onshore is the origin of the accordion sounds which are emblematic of folkloric cumbia."[18] And pretty soon lutes and guitars were added to fill out the sound. Later, cumbia became part of Colombia's 1820s independence struggle, when it was heard and seen everywhere as an expression of nationalism and civic pride.[19] Even from that, the orchestral sound of cumbia music continued to grow. Taking the cue from the Big Band Era of the 1930s, cumbia bands added saxophones and trumpets, and the pace quickened to accommodate a modern urban sensibility. Finally, cumbia bands grew to such a size that they couldn't all make the trip to tour the United States, and Puerto Rican musicians already in the United States were trained and hired. Then in the 1950s some experimented with giving cumbia an Afro-Cuban treatment. But either the recording methods were not sophisticated enough to give it wider exposure, or Colombian rhythms were too unfamiliar, and the attempt never quite caught on.[20]

Over time, and on its own, however, cumbia has adapted well to changing situations and new places in which to become popular. As a couples dance, the Latin motion of cumbia may either be demurely subdued or saucily flaunted, depending on the mood. And when danced in a group, cumbia can look a great deal like a Western swing line dance with a Latin beat to it. This is not surprising, since cumbia and Tex-Mex have been close together in their style and rhythms—in fact, Mexican musical styles have long been popular in Colombia, including mariachis.[21]

The cumbia step is easy to learn, but real finesse in the execution of it takes practice. At a snappy 2/4 pace, dancers take a step back on the right foot with a slight pivot to turn the body to the side, rock forward on the left, then step to the side with the right (pause) and repeat to the left. The visual effect presents the dancers moving in a V pattern in open holds relative to one another, allowing for swinging turns and passes. This may sound very leisurely, but the rhythm calls for a rapid step on the first three beats (a triplet) that can be performed with a slight hop (or skip), while the front-facing pause gives it a syncopated lilt. Just as the knees are flexible to give a little bit of a bounce, so too the arms are loose at the elbow, and the forearms make a slight circular motion so that a corresponding upper torso fluidity gives the dance a nice, easy flow as it rocks like a samba from side to side.[22]

Closely related to—and an influence upon—conjunto dance and music, cumbia has something of a polka feel hidden somewhere inside, induced by three quick steps and a pause. "Much of what is known as Tejano music, the contemporary music of Texas and northern Mexico made famous by Selena, is actually a pop version of cumbia."[23] But as part of the salsa phenomenon joined with Latin jazz music, cumbia has made the leap from South America to the United States fairly recently. The ever-changing chameleon skin of cumbia continues to show new colors even into the twenty-first century. Not only has cumbia melded with conjunto, but it is sometimes part of the salsa look as well. And the Texas musical group called Los Kumbia Kings performs a cumbia-rap fusion, giving cumbia ever-new and fresh surfaces, to the delight of couples deep in the Latin beat.

Conga

This easy-to-learn and broadly sociable party dance may have appeared and faded from the hottest social dance floors in the United States rather quickly. But for the short time that conga lines were in broad favor, it seemed like they were everywhere, winding along between restaurant tables, down neighborhood streets, and along tourist beaches with the conga's repetitive step-step-step-kick to the right, then repeated to the left. The Afro-Cuban conga's name is thought to be Spanish for a "Congolese woman,"[24] a dance that can be enjoyed by couples or in long lines of people single file, each with hands on the shoulders of the person in front. According to Latin music historian Isabelle Leymarie, however, " 'Conga' is said to come from a Bantu word signifying both 'song' and 'tumult.' "[25]

The conga beat (often drums and/or shakers are the only instrumental accompaniment) is a syncopated 4/4 with a step on each of the first three beats of the measure, followed by a delayed touch of the foot to either side of the direction in which the line of dancers is going. As a partnered dance, conga couples either hold hands or shine in opposition (that is, as one partner moves left, the other moves to the right in the same steps). It is a naturally friendly and welcoming dance, and Americans otherwise hesitant about Latin dancing seemed to connect with conga lines as an obvious celebratory feature. It helps to have someone knowledgeable get the dance started, something that Cuban vocalist-performer Desi Arnaz did when "he introduced the conga to America through Miami and New York, weaving through the audience as he had done as a kid in the Santiago de Cuba carnivals."[26]

But before conga was a cheerful mixer, it supported a long-standing lineage as a processional Corpus Christi and Epiphany carnival dance that was enjoyed by the politically and socially autonomous cabildos of Cuba since the 1600s. It was performed as both a serpentine and a couples dance (called a tango congo) in the streets, accompanied by a band of the loudest instruments that musicians could get their hands on—horns, drums, whistles, and even frying pans.[27]

The main musical accompaniment for conga is the drums, heartbeat of the event of dancing. While party congas in the United States some- times follow a musician leader at the front of the line keeping the beat on a pair of bongos, traditional Cuban congas were driven by a trio of drums, noticeably different than their African parent. The smallest drum, called the quinto, was a solo instrument used to introduce new rhythms. The middle-sized conga (sometimes called a tres golpes) and the larger tumba, provided the base rhythms. Modern conga drums have been reduced to two, and instead of resting on the ground, they are mounted on stands so that they can be played by a single virtuoso drummer. That way, one musician can quickly combine the more important aspects of the quinto, conga, and tumba rhythms, to produce a fairly equivalent sound of the original three-drum configuration. And the drummer is not constricted to just drumming with his hands. A polyrhythmic 6/8 pattern is sometimes incorporated into one of the conga music parts played with sticks on a hollow wooden box (cajon) or on the side of a drum.[28]

Around 1930, carnival conga came indoors, where it was transformed into a popular ballroom dance to be picked up by tourists from the United States who were on vacation. Tourists brought it—along with their versions of other Cuban dances like rhumba and mambo—back with them into the United States, and a few found a lucrative business in teaching the steps and style in social dance studios.

Conga lines are light-hearted celebrations that large groups of people can enjoy together in massed and unified dancing; at the end of World War II, long lines of celebrants wove through the main streets of every major city in the United States.

Jubilant crowd on V-J day dancing on the White House lawn. (Courtesy of the Library of Congress.)

Conga lines allow casual acquaintances or strangers to move together in a large mass, although the length of the line often breaks down when a section of it loses the beat, and there is always somebody touching to the left when everyone else is touching to the right.

But not all conga lines are meant just for celebrations or parties; congas, as an expression of protective unity and serious intent, have also appeared. In March of 1965, a group of women maintained an all-night conga line dance around a gathering of civil rights demonstrators as they slept before marching on Selma, Alabama.[29]

Mambo

Deep in the tropical Latin matrix, with its foundation firmly resting on both European danza and Afro-Cuban rhythms, lies the charanga mambo. Closely related to the cha-cha and described by some as an early partnership between American swing jazz and Cuban music, the beginnings of mambo as a modern social dance may be placed with the Victor label recording of bandleader Anselmo Sacaras' 1944 *Mambo*. Or, perhaps the honor really belongs to musician Perez Prado, who gave the music and the dance its name when he first introduced it to tourists in a performance at the Havana night club, La Tropicana, in 1943. Or, maybe it was invented when Cuban musician Antonio Arcano shifted the beat in a charanga, even though it was banned from salons and radio stations.[30]

As a type of charanga (possibly influenced by French contradanza music) which was more light on its feet than other Cuban dance music, mambo started out moving to ensembles of violins, flutes, and a vocalist backed up with percussion, piano, and bass. In the great days of ballroom mambo, the sound included a full complement of reed and horn. Almost any and all of the many varieties of percussion shakers and scrapers add to mambo's rich Afro-Latin musical texture.

But the dance has more than one style and meaning, and explanations of the origins of mambo vary between its African and Latin voices. The name is popularly supposed to have come from Haiti, where the term "mambo" refers to a voodoo priestess, just as cha-cha may have been named for the rattle used in voodoo rituals. Another possibility is that the name comes from an African drum called a mambisa. Or, it could be part of a collection of interrelated terms:

> Many Cuban musical terms, among them "conga," "bongo" and "mambo" are Congolese. "Mambo" means "prayer," "conversation with the gods," and "sacred dance." In Congo parlance, "güiri mambo" means "listen to what I have to tell you."[31]

This "listen to what I have to tell you" expression is embedded in the gesture of a raised, closed fist and a shout of "Mambo!" by the lead musician to signal the beginning of a mambo break.

Early versions of couples' mambo were pretty acrobatic, making it a dance for the young and physically fit. But this vigor was somewhat toned down, and its Afro-Cuban nature subdued, so that the mambo would appeal to white, middle-class tourists eager to try out the latest Latin dance craze, but a bit timid about loosening up the quietly vertical backbone and (horrors!) the sexualized regions of the pelvis. In that guise, mambo was taken up by dance studios faced with a decline in popularity of the rumba during the 1940s. Offering mambo lessons was a way of keeping students interested in new tropical Latin social dance sensations.

Mambo is still part of the ballroom scene, as American Rhythm DanceSport events occasionally include a mambo. However, the dance was not always a proper fit for many social dancers taking classes at dance studios, and it never became broadly popular on its own in that venue. The tempo is fairly fast, with a jerky staccato effect that is its signature characteristic with a cut-time syncopation. This is physically achieved in partnership with the music by tying a weak to a strong quick-quick-slow sequence that bridges the fourth count to the first count of the next measure.

Latin motion in a mambo is a pleasant sway of the hips side to side in the two quick counts. Adding to the challenge in performing the dance correctly is that mambo partners never sever contact with each other in open and closed holds. Some dancers find that the kind of "warm up" start of a cha-cha sequence is more "natural" for them to match with the music because it features a slow-slow, triple-quick-step pattern.[32] Even so, Rosemary Clooney singing *Mambo Italiano* (Bob Merrill; 1954), and Nat King Cole with *Papa Loves Mambo* (Perry Como; 1954) brought at least the name and the call of mambo into mainstream English vocabulary.

Still, rumba and mambo fit together rather closely in ways other than in ballroom and dance studio events. The United States popular version of the rumba features a box-style dance distinct from the mambo, which has a forward-and-back step to a quick-quick-slow musical pattern. Early mambo music was played as a rumba with a "mambo break," so that the fourth beat was accented, or in 2/4 time, so that the break punched out the second and fourth beat, whether or not the dancers—who were likely off on their own riff—were breaking with the music.

In the United States, this stronger version of mambo started out fitting in best with Harlem-mixed African-American and Latino dancers in New York City, perhaps because it became one of the dances popular for "rent parties" that were part of Harlem culture at the time. During the big band craze, mambo was king at New York City's Palladium Ballroom (among others), and in this collision between jazz and Latin music the improvisational, exhibition potential in mambo found rich expression. Still, mambo was in this frame largely danced in the Latino community; it didn't catch on with the mainstream media crowd until later.

Rhumba

Rhumba, or "rumba," depending on who is speaking. Much like cha-cha, conga, and mambo, this popular tropical Latin dance has its origins deep in Afro-Cuban culture, but as one of the de-Africanized tourist dances brought into the United States during the 1920s to 1940s. The designation "rhumba" is used to clearly distinguish the tamed-down ballroom version described here, while the stronger rumba brava is taken up in Chapter 3. In fact, some assert that the "rhumba" (like the conga) as taught in U.S. dance studios and performed as a ballroom competition dance was never really a Latin dance at all, but simply what tourists remembered from their vacations in Havana, as just about any Latin dancing was called a "rumba."[33]

In the ballroom world of rhumba, the dance is included in both the International Standard Latin Dances and American Rhythm ballroom DanceSport competitions. It can make for a seductive exhibition dance in a slow-quick-quick pattern within a moderate, unhurried tempo, with the focus on full body movements to the beat. The side-to-side traveling step is custom made for the two-dimensional view of a TV or movie camera, which captures the emotional flow between the dancing pair: "The R[h]umba is serious in its intent, a dance of passion and seduction."[34] Its characteristic rhythm is a moderate 2/4 cut time, with plenty of percussion featuring claves, drums, and maracas. Rhumba makes a nice "spot" dance that turns the dancers to face different directions, providing a pleasing change of pace for line dancing form in zumba exercises.

The name "rumba" has multiple meanings, any and all of which may apply to the dance itself. In Jamaica and Haiti, the "rumba box" (also called a marimbola) is a musical percussion instrument played for a very fast staccato sound. The word "rumboso" means flashy or showy, but a rumba is "a pile of trash." In Cuba, rumba means, "non-religious good time dance."[35] Rumba also means "to form a path" or "let's get going."[36] But in terms of the early commercialization of Latin dance music for white, middle-class consumption in the United States, the word "rumba" meant just about anything vaguely "Latin" to be danced to drums, shakers, and scrapers played by a charming group of young men in colorful shirts with lots of ruffles on their sleeves.

The image of exotic musicians carried over in the 1920s recording businesses. Both Victor and Columbia put out records of Cuban music at an increased rate, with the idea of making good sales both in the US and in the rest of Latin America. But rather than confuse non-Latin, English-speaking consumers with too many exotic terms, they put everything they could find—danzón, son, guaracha, or bolero—under the general title of "rumba."[37]

As danced today, though, rumba has reached something of a compromise between the fierce rumba brava and its tamer ballroom exhibition form to show itself as an interesting couples' dance in two forms: the Cuban rumba and the American rumba.

Overall, the Cuban rumba man preserves an air of "cool," with a subtle, controlled turn side to side for each sequence as his arms bounce up and down, slightly corresponding to the bounce in the knees. Throughout, his body is fluid and springy. His partner is very sexy, with a flowing side-to-side roll of the entire body at each step. The Latin motion of her hips is not sharp, but incorporated into the light roll of each step she takes, radiating through her torso to cause her arms and hands to follow in a corresponding flow. Ladies face front, but gentlemen turn their upper body and look in the direction of the weight shift. Each beat is a step with a roll of the body; partners do not touch, even to hold hands, which are held in front of the waist as the feet close together. With the weight transfer, arms gesture forward to the side opposite of the direction the feet are going as they move in and out.

The American rumba as taught in North American dance studios looks a bit different, though it has the same rhythm pattern as exhibition and competition rumba. This kind of rumba is a modified son (popular with middle-class Cubans), introduced by the exhibition duo of Lou Quinn and Joan Sawyer in 1913. In this version, partners maintain open and closed positions with each other. For example, in such figures as the "Aida," they dance forward and backward side by side, holding inside hands, while their outside arms are opened out with palms down, very much as if they were dancing an old-fashioned minuet. Occasionally partners will break away to do an individual outside turn (also characteristic of European court dances) before closing again in a waltz position.

However, in this version of rumba, partner torsos never touch, and their shoulders are kept quiet, features that probably helped keep the rumba barely on the inside of what might be considered more or less proper at the time of its introduction into the United States. Steps are small, and contained under the hips; the Latin motion is much subdued. Instead of weight presses side to side, as in the Cuban rumba, the basic step of American rumba is performed in a box pattern—the man steps forward as his partner steps back—and it is always achieved with a "discreet but expressive hip movement achieved by carefully timed weight transfer."[38] That means that the hip rolls slightly on the slow count (actually, just a fraction of a second before the next count) of an American rumba, in contrast to the constant rolling on each count of its Cuban cousin.

American rumba as taught in dance studios varies from a confined "spot" dance in which the partners are very closely mirroring each other's steps, to traveling steps and figures suited to exhibition dancing. While a rumba tempo remains constant, exhibition and competition rumba time signature is in 4/4. The choreography for exhibition rumba may include thrilling drops, spins, kicks, lower body twists (very showy in a well-draped dress and high heels for the ladies) and head-to-floor dips, as well as other jazz dance moves. Carriage of the upper body is very erect, giving it a look much like a tango. Steamy pauses in "iconic" poses (suited to please any photographer) allow dramatic tension to crackle between partners. "The rumba is a dance where the man shows off his partner and the woman maintains an erect and proud carriage as she moves smoothly from one figure to another."[39]

Samba

The jewel of Brazilian dances, samba is one of those foundational styles found everywhere in contemporary society, from mass media to commercials to popular social dance floors for all festive occasions. So popular did samba become that it eventually replaced the maxixie as Brazil's premier dance. Samba stands out because it is "performed with a bounce, or vertical movement of the body driven by the ankles and knees."[40]

Like many other Latin social dances, samba is versatile as a couples dance or as Rio's more well-known massed carnival processional just before Lent. Samba is, like capoeira (Brazil's fight/dance that has had such an influence on urban breaking and action movies), based on a variation of a much older dance tradition that had both sacred and secular purposes. Although long banned from urban centers for being "too African" (or, perhaps more accurately too vigorous with pelvic moves performed by both genders), the Cape Verde batuque, from which samba is derived, was part dance, part ritual, part game, and part communal identity.[41] Rio-style samba is a dance of joy and community for carnival, when Brazil is the center of the world and samba brings together its cultural diversity into one massed celebration. Samba recorded on TV is impressive—experienced firsthand, it is overwhelming. Great masses of dancers identically dressed in colors to rival a tropical garden keep up an hours-long march, held together by hundreds of drummers in a percussive explosion of sound. And everyone is so thickly packed together in the streets, it is a wonder any of them can move at all, much less play the music and dance. Today, the "Sambadome" (an area eight blocks long and one street wide) is the site at which the samba school parade groups (escolas de samba) perform.[42]

In addition to drawing masses of street dancers, samba in another form is danced by glamorous sambanistas on floats. "This samba has lightning fast, whirling steps that give the impression, when successfully done, of a mechanical eggbeater."[43] Most sambanistas are mulatas (attractive and "exotic" women who are not very black, but more like a coffee-with-cream golden color) whose fancy footwork and perfection of the pelvic gestures is matched only by the skimpiness of their costumes. While European ballroom samba deliberately mutes pelvic gesture as unaesthetic at best (and probably immoral at worst), carnival samba embraces this movement as essential to its fundamental African heritage.[44]

While the prancing, flat-footed placements of the steps are simple, samba is difficult to master, due not only to the syncopation of the beat, but also to its opposition, or isolation, movement control required of the dancer. That is, one part of the body moves in opposition to another. While the upper body is leaning in one direction, the locomotion in the feet goes in the opposite direction, or arms may gesture in one direction while the head is looking in another, etc. This distinction gives samba its pendulum, or rocking, side-to-side swaying motion through a continuous bending and straightening of the knees. Steps are short, in a characteristic "step and cut" pattern, or "step-ball-change," very close under the body weight. With that the dancers' knees produce a hip roll shift on one count. A ball-touch (in which the weight is not transferred from one foot to the other) sometimes also signals a change of direction. In all, samba exhibits the characteristic "break" of the vertical line of the body common to all tropical Latin dances in a wonderfully sculptural way.

Samba rhythm is a moderately paced, syncopated 2/4 cut time; the first count is 3/4, the second one is 1/4, and the third full count is 4/4. The dance (also called zemba, queca, zembo, or semba) is included in both American Rhythm and International Latin ballroom DanceSport competitions. Exhibition and ballroom sambas are performed in the carioca couples style that was made famous in the United States by Fred Astaire and Dolores del Rio in their 1933 MGM film, *Flying Down to Rio*. Also called the "rocking samba," carioca samba (the Carioca River runs through the city of Rio de Janeiro) was established in 1917 as a ballroom form that moves partners around the dance floor in a clockwise direction, which would allow the judges to conveniently observe each individual couple as they passed by.

A couples' dance hall samba also grew out of the versatile batuque by the end of the Eighteenth Century, as long as its "blackness" could be mitigated by European melodies and a carefully controlled Latin motion. Polkas brought to Brazil in the mid-1800s were merged with the African-based lundú, which was itself a fusion of batuque and the Iberian fandango. Despite this mixing, Brazilian samba is not often

Julia Lira, 7, dances during a rehearsal by the Viradouro samba school in Rio de Janeiro late Wednesday, February 3, 2010. (AP Photo/Felipe Dana.)

a couples' social dance in Brazil any more, though when it is danced in the nightclubs it is called Samba de Gafieira. To make matters even more confusing, neither gafieria nor the international ballroom dance samba looks anything like what is known as a samba in Brazil.

Samba as a couples' dance is not frequent in the United States, outside of competition and exhibition ballroom dance venues, for its peak of popularity hit in the 1930s and 1940 s, and samba has declined ever since. The musical accompaniment for this variety of samba had a romantic note to it, in which percussion played light background to string and wind instruments. Sometimes song lyrics were coy, even humorous, as opposed to the serious and intensely dark tragedy in tango songs.

After couples dancing declined in Rio de Janeiro, the bossa nova came closest to taking the place of the samba. But even as this "new beat" music took hold in the United States, the dance invented to go with it never quite became widely popular.[45] As the samba has gone international, it has also become a stylish couple dance in Latin clubs of every urban center, with figures such as the "twinkle," in which a twisting figure eight shows off the ladies' short, fringed skirts over long legs and feet in high heels. This version of samba provides plenty of variety in the relationship between partners. While samba pairs do dance in open "shines," the closed holds are full-body close. And its emotional direction is unmistakable: "The flow in the samba seems to begin with joy and leads to sexual awakening."[46]

Notes

1. Willie Colón, In Forward to: ¡Musica! The Rhythm of Latin America: Salsa, Rumba, Merengue, and More by Sue Steward, (San Francisco, CA: Chronicle Books, 1999), 6.

2. Sue Steward, ¡Musica! The Rhythm of Latin America: Salsa, Rumba, Merengue, and More by Sue Steward, (San Francisco, CA: Chronicle Books, 1999), 14.

3. John Charles Chasteen, National Rhythms, African Roots: The Deep History of Latin American Popular Dance (Albuquerque, NM: University of New Mexico Press, 2004), 12.

4. http://www.percussionclinic.com/ (accessed: February 28, 2010).

5. Ed Morales, The Latin Beat: The Rhythms and Roots of Latin Music from Bossa Nova to Salsa and Beyond (Cambridge, MA: Da Capro Press, 2003), 7.

6. http://www.formedia.ca/rhythms/glossary.html (accessed: March 3, 2010).

7. Steward, 9.

8. Morales, 7.

9. Morales, 8.

10. Isabelle Leymarie, Cuban Fire: the Saga of Salsa and Latin Jazz (London and New York: Continuum, 2002), 100.

11. Sue Steward, 27, 75.

12. http://web.mit.edu/rueda/www/background.html (accessed: April 27, 2010).

13. Richard M. Stephenson and Joseph Iaccarino, The Complete Book of Ballroom Dancing (Garden City, NY: Doubleday & Company, Inc., 1980), 47.

14. starlightdancestudio.com (accessed: July 2, 2009).

15. Gerald Jonas, Dancing: the Pleasure, Power, and Art of Movement (New York: Harry N. Abrams, Inc., 1998), 167.

16. Stephenson and Iaccarino, 47.

17. Leymarie, 22.

18. http://cumbiaexhibition.blogspot.com/2008/09/history.html (accessed: May 30, 2010).

19. Tijana Ilich, from http://latinmusic.about.com/od/genres/p/PRO02 BASIC.htm (accessed May 12, 2010).

20. Morales, 25.

21. Morales, 25.

22. Steward, 15.

23. Morales, 25–26.

24. www.streetswing.com/histmain/z3conga (accessed: December 5, 2009).

25. Leymarie, 17.

26. Steward, 31–33.

27. Leymarie, 22.

28. http://www.formedia.ca/rhythms/glossary.html (accessed: March 3, 2010).

29. *New York World-Telegram* at: http://www.loc.gov/rr/print/res/076 _nyw.html (accessed: January 4, 2010).

30. Steward, 35.

31. Leymarie, 17.

32. Stephenson and Iaccarino, 46–47.

33. Steward, 31–33.

34. Reynolds, 43.

35. Stephenson and Iaccarino, 43.

36. Morales, 10.

37. Steward, 49.

38. Stephenson and Iaccarino, 44.

39. Stephenson and Iaccarino, 119.

40. Yvonne Marceau, "Ballroom Dance Competition," In Selma Jeanne Cohen, Ed. *International Encyclopedia of Dance*, Vol. 1 (New York: Oxford University Press, 1999), 358–359.

41. Morton Marks, "Brazil, Ritual and Popular Dance," In Selma Jeanne Cohen, Ed. *International Encyclopedia of Dance*, Vol. 1 (New York: Oxford University Press, 1999), 527.

42. Chasteen, 8.

43. Chasteen, 9.

44. Stephenson and Iaccarino, 6.

45. Chasteen, 9.

46. Reynolds, 43.

3

That Latin Beat: How Latin Dance and Music Got into the United States

I grew up in a neighborhood where there were only Dominicans, Puerto Ricans, and Haitians. My roots are from Africa, my father's side is Dominican, and my mom is Honduran. My family comes from the Ibo tribe from West Africa. I feel so connected to hear the sounds of the drums!

Mitchell Marks[1]

It is on the Latin social dance floor that each dancer proclaims identity, origin, and significance—past, present and future: "I am Cuban/ Puerto Rican/Dominican, and I live in the United States." Here we have a look at how Latin dances came into the United States and how their new setting changed them. Culturally, it is about first-generation immigration from Caribbean islands into New York City, Miami, and Los Angeles due to war, revolution, and industrialization from the 1800s into the 1900s. And tucked in with hopes and dreams of a better life, new arrivals also brought Latin dances and music made sturdy from the rural countryside, brushed up into urban sophistication in Havana or Buenos Aires, and framed in distinct national identities.

As "naturalized citizens" of our contemporary culture, Latin dances became a significant part of collaborative experimentation across many different—and maybe a few surprising—popular U.S. music and social dance genres already caught up in their own changes. Latin music is influenced by Spanish song forms, African-Amerindian rhythms and harmonic structures, and European classical and popular music, so fusion is at the core of what goes into Latin dances. Having already brought together European and non-European motifs, Latin dances provide stylistic bridges between groups of people in the United States—a little that is familiar mixed with a little that is unfamiliar. Increasingly in the twentieth and twenty-first centuries, Latin music also makes some amazing exchanges with North American ballad, rhythm & blues, jazz, rock, reggae, electronica, rap, Afro-pop and hip-hop—just to name a few. And they all fit together as American sound, from the seventeenth to the twentieth century:

> The Americas and the Caribbean islands were colonized with an immense blending of race, language, religion and music. Latin music we hear today mostly originates from the rhythms African slaves brought to the new world.[2]

The especially potent combination of African-American dance and music with Latin cultures creates a rich variety that brings together diverse people on one dance floor under a primary rhythm. And wherever the music goes, there go the dances: left, right and sideways. But however far they go, and in whatever way they change, the binding factor among them remains the repeating clave beat; unmistakably irresistible from New York City to Los Angeles and everywhere in between.

With all this shifting around, it isn't easy to keep track of separate styles, or their countries of origin. Sometimes dances of the same name are entirely different along racial and socioeconomic lines. Mambo, tango, and rumba are split in this way, with one style associated with the Latin American tourist trade, while an entirely different kind of dance goes on behind the scenes, off-limits to the average tourist as part of the Afro-Latin tradition. Instead, night club show reviews featured "overflowing bowls" of elaborately-dressed women who could move in alluring ways, and when visitors and tourists tried out some of the dances, they brought them—conga, rhumba, cha-cha, and mambo—back to the United States as a collective Latin bundle called "rhumbas."[3] Conversely, just a quick leap off Cuba brought musicians into the United States to lay the foundations for one of history's most remarkable musical transformations.

The chorus line at the Tropicana nightclub in Havana on February 6, 1956. (AP Photo.)

Several distinct stages mark the passage of Latin dancing from folk to social dance status. Phase one is the transition from being local folk events that tourists find quaint and picturesque into national and international dances. Tropical Latin dances like mambo and rumba brava provide examples of this phase. Next, the musical developments of ragtime to jazz during the late 1800s into the early 1900s in the United States open the door to the tango craze and tango teas. Facilitated by a breakdown of class divisions on the dance floor through wholesale urbanization, immigration, and industrialization in that period paves the way to leaving the dictates of ballroom dancing masters and the popularity of dance halls fed by the daring dances of jook (juke) joints and honky-tonks.

From Folk to Social Dance: Mambo and Rumba Brava

The love of dance is never more ingrained in any culture of the world than it is in Latin America. The sheer variety of folk dances from South and Central America, the Caribbean, and Mexico is dazzling; the music explores every nuance of feeling, and the Spanish language fires song lyrics from mournful love ballads to impassioned calls to social justice. The power of language and its tie to music is evident in that the first American printed music book in 1556 was published in Mexico City. Since there is a direct line from regional folk and national dances to international Latin, listed here are the Latin countries, their languages, and the names of several (though by no means all) of the more well-known folk and national dances from which social dances have benefitted:

Spain	Spanish	flamenco fandango sevillana seguidillas zapateo bolero
Mexico	Spanish	jarana huapango jarabe (19th Cent. national dance) European court dances
Argentina	Spanish, English	malambo escondido pericón chamamé tango
Bolivia	Spanish	takirari
Brazil	Portuguese	chamarrita capoeira samba batuque lundú
Puerto Rico	Spanish	bomba plena
Cuba	Spanish	conga rumba cha-cha son-montuno
Haiti	Creole French	kombit Vodun dances
Dominican Republic	Spanish	bachata merengue serembo guarapo tumba (quadrille)
Colombia	Spanish	mestizada seis-ocho baile(s) cumbia

The decades-long transition from folk dances of the Caribbean countryside and towns to social dances in urban centers of the United States is a complex journey. First, the codification of each style identifies the dance despite local variations in rural communities. Second, dances that resonate with a balance between novelty and familiarity between rural and urban groups within the country of origin (as would be the case for dances with nationalistic or ritualistic commonalities) are the ones that survive the move from country to city.

Then, dances are split between tourist and indigenous versions, and brought into the United States. While some of the tourist versions were promoted by dance studios and evolved into ballroom styles, indigenous versions came into the big cities with immigrants. Out of a combination of Latin and African-American influences at work in the United States, these dances hit their heydays during the eras of the big bands and disco, as Latinos identified with mainstream and media images, and the labor force brought factory workers elbow-to-elbow with one another across ethnic and racial barriers.

Finally, in the midst of a resurgence of ethnic identity among second-generation Nuyoricans (New York Puerto Ricans) speaking both English and Spanish, Latin dance and music assume the tools of mass media and culture—not to fit into them—but to make them serve the Latin spirit. This new dance club venue welcomes any dancer attracted to the Latin beat through jazz. And the hyper-Latin style of salsa covers just about anything from merengue to cha-cha to mambo to bachata to—well, you name it; they'll dance it. The general journey is the story of the mambo, rumba brava, and tango, which are the dances discussed here.

The most thorough cultural mixing and mingling of social dance styles takes place in port cities which tended to gather in—and accept—a variety of cultures represented not only by individuals, but by sizable groups of immigrants displaced by economic changes, civil war, or revolution. Large shipping port cities such as Buenos Aires, Argentina; Havana, Cuba; New York City; and New Orleans are usually the first locations of social dance transformations. Just as ships import and export goods and resources from all over the world through these port cities, they also bring in and send out cultural traditions that mix and meld, creating new, fresh, and vigorous dances. Language, religious practices, and music and dance not only provide a source of unity and identification with the mother country, but serve as a source of pride and distinction for a minority.

These port cities of the United States are locations in which the distinctly North American musical innovation of jazz evolved. For New York City, this was the famed "five corners" area in which some of the poorest immigrants from Italy and Ireland, as well as the newly-freed African-Americans, flocked in the late 1800s and early 1900s. While these groups fought and struggled against each other in poverty, they also exchanged dance moves that eventually evolved into East Coast style jazz (related to, but not quite the same as New Orleans jazz) and tap dancing.

A strong pull moving folk dances out of the local countryside into international and urban contexts was the relationship between the dance itself and its music. Especially during the first half of the last century, Latin music and dance had just enough of the unfamiliar melded with the familiar to offer the mainstream-middle-class social dancers a tinge of the exotic without being directly confrontational: "Latin music, like Latin American culture, comes across as exotic to North American and European listeners, with its vaguely 'hot' rhythms and emotional vocalists."[4]

But the world has changed tremendously in the last half of the 1900s, most dramatically through the global "web" connections of the Internet and international commerce. While modernism separates functions and groups of people along cultural lines, the postmodern world view incorporates many different (and often opposing) points of view simultaneously. Latin dance and music is right in the middle of this cultural process, not only finding its way in this new North American cultural "soup," but positively flourishing in it. And the racial divide between European and African music quickly broke down, mediated by Latin:

> Latin America's national rhythms were often *transgressive*. They somehow *crossed* a "color line." Because they mixed African and European styles, they introduced black culture into white society.[5]

Once Latin music got a toehold into the urban nightlife of U.S. dance clubs, there was no stopping it. And the lure of the clave didn't just go out to Euro-Americans. The ensemble Orquesta de la Luz, started in 1988, is entirely made up of Japanese musicians with a female vocalist—Nora Shiji, who sings flawlessly in Spanish—even though none of them actually speaks Spanish, and they learned the songs, the sounds, and the music from listening to recordings.[6]

Immediately after World War II, the South Bronx of New York City became a center of Latin dances with mambo, samba, and eventually, salsa. The American Routes program has featured the music of Latin Jazz great Tito Puente in "Beat of the Boroughs" because this music has become a defining feature of the city.[7] And the spoken/sung language is Spanish; the partnership between music and dance with song lyrics in the United States was never closer than between Latin music and dances right from the very beginning.

Mambo is one of the best examples of the Afro-Latin meld that went off to the United States and did well there. In Cuba, mambo grew out of a souped-up charanga danzón that had added a vocalist, which became a huge sensation around the world in the early 1940s. With short melodic phrases repeated over each time in a new variation of the original tune, the whole thing turned "sideways," opening the preordained patterns of danzón music to climactic improvisations, which in turn had the effect of prodding dance couples to do the same. While the controversy of who first invented mambo is still debated, it is clear that it became mambo when it took on a bigger sound, with the addition of flute and piano solos, backed up with bass and other strings, timbales and conga drums, and a cowbell. Likely the credit for the invention goes to several Cuban "cooks" who made mambo "sabrosura," or "tasty"—Antonio Arcano, Arsenio Rodríguez, Pérez Prado, and the López brothers, who were part of Arcano's danzón orchestra on cello, piano, and double bass. So maybe it is no surprise the "tasty" mambo hit New York City's South Bronx night clubs and dance clubs in a big way after World War II, and then (following the disco period) became part of the salsa sensation of the 1980s.

Mambo became the dance of choice in Harlem and the Bronx for rent parties, an institution that helped families cope with unemployment and housing shortages between the wars. Rent parties that included dances had been a convention in the 1920s among African-American urban communities. They were designed to raise money to meet the rent each month—something African American families had a much harder time doing than their white counterparts. Rent parties were variously called chittlin' struts, house shouts, or Blue Monday Affairs, a kind of aid-society approach. Money was raised via selling tickets, and the events included drinking, eating, dancing, music, and some gambling. Besides the enjoyment of dancing, black musicians—who had few opportunities to play in professional venues—honed their skills and

Winners of the weekly Monday night mambo contest—Lee Moates from New York and Tonita Malau from Brooklyn—dance during their performance at the Savoy Ballroom in the Harlem neighborhood of New York City on April 24, 1953. (AP Photo.)

learned from each other new ways in which to push the music at these events. Some even made a fair living out of it, performing on the "rent shout circuit" for a good meal and all the liquor they could drink. Rent parties were where musicians like Fats Waller (1904–1943) and Duke Ellington (1899–1974) got their starts.[8] But it still left African American artists to one side of the socioeconomic divide.

And the mambo—its music and the dance—was also split along racial and economic lines. Consider the story of its origins; one version of how mambo social dance music in Cuba was first officially introduced in 1943 says that it was by bandmaster Perez Prado at La Tropicana, a swanky Havana night club.[9] But mambo dancing in places like La Tropicana, where wealthy tourists gathered was nothing like mambo dancing at New York City's Palladium Ballroom.

Originally a dance studio, the Palladium dance hall on the second floor at 53rd and Broadway accommodated close to a thousand dancers at a time. Latin bands honed their skills at Spanish Harlem night clubs like The Conga, Park Plaza or China Doll, then started playing the afternoon matinee set at the Palladium when the owner realized he could jumpstart his failing investment by opening it to blacks, Puerto Ricans, and Cuban dancers. The first 1948 Sunday Latin set was a sensation, and before long, masses of young mambo dancers were showing up to vie with one another for prizes every Wednesday. Although the improvisational moves of mambo couples made the place famous, other styles of Latin dances like merengue, pachanga, and cha-cha were also favorites. But mambo had the thrill of competition and allowed for all kinds of virtuoso displays of dance skills on the part of each of the two partners, in turn. Together, the whole thing began to look very much like a jitterbug mixed with modern, ballet, and other kinds of show dancing taken to the hilt of each couples' exhibition capacity.

Wednesday nights also attracted novice mamboistas because a free dance lesson was provided. From 1948 to 1966, Palladium was the hotspot for crowds of young Latino and African-American couples—not to mention a movie star or two from time to time. The music of Latin greats such as vocalist Celia Cruz, Tito Rodriguez (1923–1973), Machito (1909–1984; born as Francisco Raúl Gutiérrez Grillo), and Tito Puente went on nonstop from one group to the next, and the dancers never seemed to get tired of it. Puerto Rican stars Ismael Rivera and Rafael Cortijo were so popular that: "...schools eventually closed down when they played free concerts because students never returned from their lunch breaks."[10]

But the golden reign of mambo ended in 1966 as the Palladium lost its liquor license and was shut down. And when Cuban musicians couldn't move freely between the United States and Havana with the advent of communism, fresh new Latin music stalled, leaving first-generation, bi-lingual Latinos ("Nuyoricans") to filled the void. And fill it they did—between mainstream mass media and Latin cultures with a galaxy of Latin pop variations that did indeed cross over with a mambo root system. These included the dengue, jala jala, shing-a-ling and boogaloo (bugalú), which were all mambo/cha-cha offshoots. Then this kind of charanga/jazz bond ended in 1969, leaving an opening for yet another American Latin fusion that is still going strong today: salsa.[11]

Like mambo, rumba brava roots are deeply entrenched in slave dancing, and the two dances are closely connected—"fraternal twins," you might say—because one form of rumba became the version of mambo that succeeded so brilliantly in the United States.

Authentic rumba is sometimes called rumba brava to separate it from the tourist version. Nightclub routines regularly featured rumba music for floor shows and social dancing, which the paying public liked, so "several Cuban singers have built their careers singing rumba and other Afro-Cuban religious music in commercial settings."[12] The international hit tune, *El Manisero* (The Peanut Vendor) further spread that version of the dance. But while happy tourists were busy rhumbaing the night away in luxury hotels to music provided by well-dressed, pass-for-white musicians, rumba brava had already been a long-standing tradition in places that tourists rarely found; the bars, dance halls, and private parties of swelling ghettos in every major city.

Rumba brava was a creation of slave dancing that made its way from the rural setting of plantations and into the laboring populations of the busy port city of Havana during the 1800s. As such, it made the authorities nervous over its frankly African approach to movements between men and women and the way its call-and-response relationship between drummers and the dancers tested skill and endurance. Sometimes a waving scarf provided a metaphor for the movements of the hips, though fluttering hands and shaking shoulders provided a connection to its origins in an African fertility dance. The term "rumba" not only applies to the dance, but also to the clave beat usually rounded out with the cata (a cane-like stick) and the maranga (an iron rattle) that drives the dancers.[13]

In the first decade of the 1900s, Cuban rumberos, or groups of musicians who consistently play together, started up from mutual-aid societies. These societies were nothing new, nor were they just a mechanism of the independent, self-governing Cabildos—mutual-aid societies have been active all over the world and in most cultures.

Out of many local variations, three main sub-styles of rumba brava traditionally led by three congas and/or a cajon evolved. Yambu rumba is sad; the singer wails out the song, and the movements are said to be paced at a tempo for "old people dancing" with little or no Latin motion to it; it is described as being more dignified than anything else, and probably has the closest connection with Spanish dance influences. It is in the Yambu rumba that the cajon player shines brightest.

Rumba columbia is played in a 6/8 time signature, and sung with a combination of Spanish and African phrases out of the Afro-Cuban culture that moved into the urban social dance scene of Havana.[14] There, it turned into the classic mambo of the 1950s and 1960s that hit the U. S. east coast scene, and merged yet again into a strong African-American urban social dance tradition. Columbia is set at the fastest tempo, and encourages the male dancer to step out in breakneck moves in fairly short bursts of sequence, not unlike "house" dancing or street break dances in U.S. city dance clubs. The vocal accompaniment is call and response by other participant/observers surrounding the performer, who must show his skill in moving all parts of his body in different ways, an arrangement that calls to mind a stylistic connection with capoeira.[15]

The guaguancó rumba moved from its Latin roots into the urban North American social dance scene, where it became popular as rumba brava. Frankly sexual, this couples' dance features a spectacular grinding pelvic movement between partners called vacunao (literally "vaccine," although it might make more sense related to the Spanish word "vacuno" or cattle), bringing this rumba brava style in comparison to a more recent version of reggaeton. Danced inside a circle of participant/observers, pairs of dancers take turns, accompanied by stringed instruments for the melody and three different kinds of drums for the base rhythm in 6/8 time. But the middle conga drum (tres golpes) also sets up a polyrhythmic 4/4 tension, lending this form of rumba brava particularly to the development of salsa.[16]

Ragtime and Jazz

Both Latin music and dance are mixed breeds, just as any genuine American art must be. The first serious concert composer and virtuoso pianist of the United States fit this requirement handily. He was Louis Moreau Gottschalk (1829–1869), born and raised in New Orleans of a Seraphic Jewish father from England and a mother who was French-Haitian. A brilliant pianist, Gottschalk toured all over the world as a celebrity virtuoso, and he was so good at it that he even made the famed European pianist Franz List (1811–1886) rather nervous because aristocratic women of all ages had a tendency to swoon at Gottchalk's concerts; or, at least, that was his reputation.

As well as performing the works of others in the finest salons of the rich and the aristocracy, Gottschalk composed and played in a piano style he called "pianola," which probably acted as a bridge between the respectability of classical music and the unacceptable but exciting syncopations of "low class" popular tunes of the day. This bridge no doubt paved the way for "ragtime" (or, "ragged music") with its pounding "stride" piano to gain widespread popularity in the United States. He also enthusiastically joined in nationalist sentiments, as South America struggled to overcome the shadow of colonialism, and he sought to make his music serve that impulse of revolution.[17]

Ragtime music is the undisputed "grandfather" of modern American piano jazz. It appeared near the start of the twentieth century as played in urban saloons, dancehalls, bars, brothels, and cafes. But this music style that set feet tapping never stayed in one place very long. The most well-known composer of ragtime tunes was Scott Joplin (1868–1917), whose 1899 *Maple Leaf Rag* was the first instrumental sheet music to sell a million copies. The mass publication of sheet music landed on pianos in many well-to-do parlors, and ragtime tunes kicked up the pace of private gatherings right alongside of Italian art songs. In addition, ragtime hitched a ride all across the United States with touring minstrel shows, which often concluded with a rousing performance of a high-stepping couples "cakewalk."

When the minstrel shows faded out to the new itinerant entertainment of vaudeville, ragtime music fell right into the new format, spreading its oddly familiar, yet oddly exotic syncopation. The secret of ragtime's bridge lay in the way it related to European 2/4 marches with a snappy melodic syncopation—bringing the note in a little early or delaying its sound perhaps by half a beat on the right hand, while the left hand kept the base beat steady.[18]

Ragtime was the music of a different dance environment, a cheap entertainment for the working classes of people who fit into a small, often dark dance floor together, instead of spreading out across a large, chandelier-lit ballroom. They could, in fact, be crammed onto tiny dance floors like bats in caves, which some of the cheap dance halls patronized by factory workers actually were. And pretty soon, ragtime shifted into a new mode that was to become jazz, which has "a tendency to stress the weak (second and fourth) beats of the bar in contrast to traditional music, which stressed the first and third beats,"[19] a trait inherited from ragtime.

The steps to the dances that went with this kind of music were quick and easy to learn. A novice pair could watch an experienced couple dancing and then try it out right there and then, without the expense of hiring a dancing master to teach it. The modern sensibilities of the younger generation were framed in terms of this music. Urban, sophisticated, and contemptuous of the tyrannies of tradition, these youngsters were the ones who, through public education, began to look to their peers rather than to the authorities of parents or teachers for tips on how to define themselves as modern young adults.

Social dancing stepped right into the mass media culture of advertizing as well. As the movies and later television showed these dances, youngsters could practice in the privacy of their own bedrooms, and diagrams of the latest steps ran in the magazines right next to the latest in toothpaste or hair cream products. The polyglot lineage of these dances also offered ample opportunity for improvisation and exchange; there was no one single way of dancing, and class lines blurred in the general acceleration of the pace of city life. True, dance studios quickly stepped into the void inhabited by the timid or rhythmically challenged, and the more successful of them (such as the Arthur Murray and Astaire Studios) franchised the business of teaching social dances all over the United States. Latin dances remain popular in them even today, whether or not ballroom competition is in mind. After all, there are social events of all kinds going on that call for some basic skill in social dancing—receptions celebrating marriages, anniversaries, bar or bat mitzvahs, school dances, block parties, etc.

Not only did the new social dance suggested by ragtime music do away with expensive dancing masters and grand ballrooms, but it did away with the need to buy expensive ball gowns and suits, gloves, and special shoes. The modern girl bobbed her hair and raised her hemlines; out went swaths of fabric and laced-up corsets in favor of a sleek, Art Deco profile. Instead of gliding and whirling smoothly around the dance floor in a waltz, couples squeezed in closely, cheek-to-cheek with one another to hop, kick, or step on every piston-pounding beat of a dance song. Idiosyncratic dances performed side by side, like the Charleston, let knees go double-jointed knocky, while elbows jutted out and hands snapped out or described window-washing circles in the air.

Parents could wail, and church ministers could tear their hair out all they liked over the impropriety of the new dance craze, but it did no good. Not even making the girls wear bumper belts[20] to keep partners from getting too close in the torso did much good (the girls just took them off, as they had earlier with their corsets when they arrived at the dance). That beat had the ear of the younger generation, like the allure of a new automobile, and nothing was going to stop it. It was the Jazz Age, looking forward to a new ground on which to dance.

And ragtime music merging into jazz opened the door for Latin dances to step out into the dance frenzy that was seizing the United States of the early 1900s.

From Argentine Tango to Tango Teas

One Latin dance in particular, the tango, caught on among the elite. Whether African, French, Spanish, English, or a melding of all the above, the tango was a mysterious dance of indeterminate origins and questionable morality—features that made it all the more attractive to upper-class ladies who patronized the infamous "tango teas" around 1910 to 1914 (or so).

Like its close relative the maxixie, and the briefly-popular lambada, tango has, right from the beginning, enjoyed the notoriety of being a "forbidden" dance, especially in the United States and Europe. Its full-body contact between partners continually outraged middle-class morality right on through most of the first half of the twentieth century. "In 1913, if German army or navy personnel danced the tango, they could have been dismissed."[21] In 1930, two dances topped the list of those most frequently condemned as immoral—the turkey trot and the tango. It could also be hazardous; several deaths (including that of a 102-year-old man, a week after his first tango lesson) and broken bones have been blamed on the tango.[22]

The story of how the tango developed into the dance it is today is vague, and even reliable accounts disagree. It seems to have (possibly) started from a dance of Andalusia, Spain, in the early 1800s, which was performed by a single woman dancing alone—a chachuca. A little later, it became a dance performed by two people walking together; this ambiguous description of a proto-tango kind of dancing is certainly plausible, given that the tango is sometimes described as an elaborate sort of "walking together," and not exclusively by a man and a woman, but sometimes by partners of the same gender. Yet another proposed theory on the origin of the tango states that it started as a street fight between two men over a woman, a narrative in which it meets up with the violent Parisian nightclub exhibition dance (which tittered the tourists) of the first decade of the twentieth century, known as the apache.

Never a dance of the same time and place, some form of proto-tango dancing probably came into the New World via Spain and then returned to Spain and France around the turn of the century—much changed by black and creole rhythms. But although there are different accounts of how the dance got there, most everyone agrees it became the tango in Argentina, as part of a growing urban underground culture centered close to the port docks of Buenos Aires during the 1800s. It grew up in several places, including the Barrio de las Ranas (literally, the Frog District), and "the downtown district of Corientes, the site of many dance halls and nightclubs."[23] And although we think of Buenos Aires as the tango's birthplace, the smaller city of Montevidio, Uruguay, which lies across the Rio de la Plata from Buenos Aires, also sported a thriving tango culture.[24]

Wherever it was danced, tango was called the baile con corté, or "dance with a stop," although the word corté means "cut." In fact, any time signature or style of dance performed with a stop was called a tango—even if the steps were those of a waltz. Its music was provided by a German accordion and the voice of the singer; in time, violins, piano, and bass were added for what came to be regarded as the "classical" tango sound.

Argentine port cities where tango flourished were cosmopolitan and welcoming to many different kinds of people—from within and without. The mixed immigrant culture was composed of the dispossessed of indeterminate parentage who ended up there from all parts of the world: shippers, sailors, merchants, service people of all kinds, prostitutes, and artists—not the least of whom were touring performers of the Lyric Theatre zarzuela, who may also have brought the essence of the tango with them.[25] And there were many European ethnic groups pouring their nostalgic hearts into tango music: Italians, Jews, Germans, French, and English, just to name a few. In Buenos Aires they came together in a vigorous intellectual artistic community, at once cosmopolitan and sophisticated as an international center:

> Buenos Aires was almost its own separate culture from the rest of Argentina: its university (opened in 1821) free of church control set the port city as an intellectual center as well as the point of import of European culture and luxuries. . . . A resident opera company was founded in 1848 in Buenos Aires, and ballet was performed as early as the 1830s.[26]

Even gauchos from the great Argentine and Uruguayan plains, who had been abruptly displaced, moved into the teeming portside culture. While the Argentine "cowboy" or gaucho probably didn't invent the tango, it is likely that many gauchos ended up in Buenos Aires and contributed to the evolution of the dance. The golden age of the Argentine gaucho was brief. By 1880 most of them had been conscripted into the army, consigned to work on a ranch owned by some wealthy European who didn't live there, or had fled to the slums of Buenos Aires, where they mixed with other displaced men collectively called guapos (pretty boys) or compadritos (tough guys). There is some evidence that gaucho song lyrics and melodies got taken up as tango tunes; these solo balladeers with guitars were called payadores, and their music could earn them a bit to live on, more or less. So in a sense, the gauchos entered the world of tango after they had given up being gauchos.[27]

Not all compadritos were common riffraff; some were well educated, verbally witty, and working at regular jobs. Some ran counterintelligence operations while serving as cab drivers. They were of mixed race—belonging to no class or family—and cultivated a pride in their own subcultural identity, almost like the beatniks of the late 1940s to early 1950s in the United States. They were freethinking, even if they sometimes worked for the boss, or otherwise skinned through periods of unemployment with some not-quite-legal activities. Compadritos had their own manner of dress, kept their own hours, had their own haunts, and even developed their own language, Lunfardo (meaning, "thieves' slang").[28]

Lunfardo was originally a patois (Fr: meaning to "paw roughly"—a non-standard local language) of the minor criminal class and became the expressive language of choice for writers of symbolic and metaphoric tango lyrics. The Spanish word literately suggests a melding of "lun[e]" (moon) and "fardo" (a bundle or pack), which works very well with the idea of thieves carrying around their bundles of loot by moonlight. It is a dark and dense language appropriate to the tango; for example, the Lunfardo word "mufarse" means "the pleasure of wallowing in one's own gloom." "Song of a far away land/that idealizes the dirty tavern/ and that shines in the eyes of the Italian/as the pearl of a tear"—so go the lyrics of the tango song *La Violeta*.[29]

It does, as they say, "take two to tango," and the female companion to a compadrito was called the mina, who was "an unmarried woman who was usually attached to one man at a time, but who filled in the time between attachments with prostitution." The mina, according to the early tango songs, was doomed to betray her man—either to the authorities for money, or by cheating on him with another man.[30] Knife fights (whether over a woman or some other issue) were common; for every five men there was one woman in Buenos Aires of the late 1800s. But tango dance sometimes served to displace the deadliness of the violence that often erupted between Creole natives and newly-arrived immigrants (often Italian):

> Eventually, the tango replaced the knife. This ritualization of conflict suggests another interpretation for the phenomenon of men dancing the tango together: perhaps the tradition grew as much out of conflict resolution as out of teaching and competitive performing.[31]

Tango might have remained local to Argentina had it not been for two upper-class changes in the first decade of the Twentieth Century. For one thing, tango hitched a trip to Paris with the wealthy sons of Argentine businessmen, who had been sent to Europe to "sow their wild oats" before settling down (so to speak), and maybe obtain a little European polish into the bargain. At around the same time, Americans were also arriving in Paris on vacation, particularly driven there by the restraints of Prohibition at home. Parisians and Argentine émigrés were very willing to cash in on the tango craze. "By 1913, there were reportedly a hundred Argentines giving tango lessons in Paris," and it didn't stay there; by 1912 the tango had also been introduced into England, and spread from there to Germany.[32]

Tango was an immediate sensation; it was a novelty to European dancers for a couples dance to include some degree of improvisation. Not to mention that the close hold, thigh-to-thigh contact, and deep lunges that might allow the lady's skirt to rise above the knees (even if she was wearing tights) added to the exotic allure of the dance. Tango, with all its flair and promise of sensuous passion, officially arrived in the United States from Paris early in 1911 with an exhibition performance by dancer Maurice Mouvet (1888–1927) and his partner at Louis Martin's in Manhattan.

Mouvet had learned the tango at an early age in Paris while visiting there with his father, but when the popularity of the dance blossomed in the United States, he set up to teach it to anyone who would pay $25 an hour for instruction.[33] Mouvet had a knack for creating the suitable link that made disreputable dances fashionably acceptable to a large social dance crowd. He is credited with not only introducing and encouraging the popularity of the tango in the United States, but also tango's Brazilian cousin, the maxixie, and a crude Paris cabaret dance known as the apache.[34]

When the dance team of Vernon and Irene Castle also performed or taught the maxixie or the tango—and in the process removed Mouvet himself as the premier standard of good taste in Latin dancing—they did make a clear distinction between the two dances. But for most amateur dancers that wasn't necessarily the case. It is this mix of dances that seems to have provided Jazz Age writer F. Scott Fitzgerald (1896–1940) with a standard of superficial chic in several of his novels, where such dancing is collectively identified as the maxixie. And Americans who could afford to take lessons in Paris themselves—in anything that might pass for a tango—were eager to be the first of their social circles to show off the latest moves.[35]

Regardless of what it was called, the tango was performed to habanera music and got swept up into the general peak of the dance craze of 1913–1914, whereupon it was almost instantly branded as immoral:

> In Atlantic City, New Jersey, Mrs. Lillian Albers, soloist of the St. Paul's Methodist Episcopal Church Choir received an ultimatum: stop teaching the Tango or resign from the church. She resigned immediately.[36]

Tango entered a new phase in the social dance scene of the United States in 1912 when "Tango Tea" afternoons became popular, especially in New York City. When the Waldorf Hotel was built in 1908, tango teas were advertized almost as soon as the tango had arrived from Paris, as announced in the *Dancing Times*: "The 'Tango' is graceful, decorous and worthy of a place in any ballroom. If you doubt me, go to one of the 'Thés Dansants' organized by the Boston Club on Wednesday afternoons at The Waldorf Hotel, and you will be charmed. (June, 1913)."[37]

Tango teas were almost entirely a feminine phenomenon, unique to that time period, although a graceful nostalgia for times gone by has resurrected "Tango Teas" as a contemporary pleasure. At the peak of their popularity around 1914, tango teas provided a way for bored society women to indulge in romantic fantasy. Very little about a tango tea was "real"; the success of these events depended upon a vivid imagination and a desire for the safe "thrill" suggested by romance fiction. The tea they drank wasn't always "tea" (according to the memoirs of one of the men who worked in a tea parlor, there was more rum than anything else in those teacups). But the dance—even tamed down—had that foreign, exotic tinge to it that sent feminine pulses racing in ways that their dull, mercantile, and obsessively-busy-making-money husbands could not imagine. Society women flocked to lavishly-decorated tea parlors all over the city. There they paid the admission price for a leisurely afternoon of socializing and dancing the tango with "professional men" of indeterminate origins. These men were sometimes critically termed "tango pirates," "lounge lizards" or later, "gigolos" who also offered romantic favors.[38]

As the fad faded (aided no doubt, by several blackmail attempts and the shift of the dance craze to idiosyncratic dances like the Charleston), tango teas ceased to be popular. But the dark and slightly dangerous Latin male as a romantic icon continued to flutter feminine pulses; a fact early moviemakers did not overlook.

Ballet dancer Rudolph Nureyev as Rudolf Valentino with Christine Charlson, August 1976. (AP Photo.)

The most famous movie icon of this kind was the Italian-American Rudolf Valentino (Ruodolfo Guglielmi). With his dark, slicked-back hair, slender physique, limpid (some said hypnotic) bedroom eyes, and smoldering cinema passion, Valentino provided a general-purpose exotic flair, whether as an Arabian prince or a tango-dancing Latin lover. Even today, tango retains an aloof and separate aura, as tango dancers of the twenty-first century all over the world disdain the mass-media appeal of other social Latin dances. At the same time, anyone—of any age—can learn and enjoy the subtle variations and grace of the dance, whether through ballroom dance instruction at a dance studio, or through the many tango dance groups ongoing in any city of the United States.

Notes

1. Mitchell Marks, Seattle Latin club dancer: interview Apr 27, 2010.

2. http://www.formedia.ca/rhythms/glossary.html (accessed: March 3, 2010).

3. Sue Steward, ¡Musica! The Rhythm of Latin America: Salsa, Rumba, Merengue, and More (San Francisco, CA: Chronicle Books, 1999), 31.

4. Ed Morales, The Latin Beat: The Rhythms and Roots of Latin Music from Bossa Nova to Salsa and Beyond (Cambridge, MA: Da Capro Press, 2003), Introduction.

5. John Charles Chasteen, National Rhythms, African Roots: The Deep History of Latin American Popular Dance (Albuquerque, NM: University of New Mexico Press, 2004), 5.

6. Steward, 71.

7. http://www.americanroutes.publicradio.org (accessed: January 27, 2010).

8. Katarina Hazzard-Gordon, Jookin': The Rise of Social Dance Formations in African-American Culture (Philadelphia, PA: Temple University Press, 1990), 116–117.

9. http://theboweryboys.blogspot.com/2007/11/friday-night-fever-palladium -ballroom.html (accessed: June 12, 2010).

10. Steward, 99.

11. Steward, 60.

12. Steward, 31.

13. Morales, 10.

14. Morales, xx.

15. http://www.purelistener.com/e/music/cuba-1.html (accessed: June 5, 2010).

16. http://www.formedia.ca/rhythms/glossary.html (accessed: March 3, 2010).

17. Chasteen, 2.

18. Richard M. Stephenson and Joseph Iaccarino, The Complete Book of Ballroom Dancing (Garden City, NY: Doubleday & Company, Inc., 1980), 24.

19. Stephenson and Iaccarino, 37.

20. Ralph G. Giordano, *Social Dancing in America: Lindy Hop to Hip Hop, 1901–2000*, Vol. 2 (Westport, CN and London: Greenwood Press, 2007), 72.

21. Susie Hodge, *Dance: Latin and Ballroom* (Chicago, IL: Heinemann Library, 2008), 17.

22. Jo Baim, *Tango: Creation of a Cultural Icon* (Bloomington and Indianapolis, IN: Indiana University Press, 2007), 56.

23. Baim, 17.

24. Chasteen, 18.

25. Stephenson and Iaccarino, 5.

26. Baim, 15.

27. Morales, 28–29.

28. Baim, 3.

29. Baim, 40.

30. Baim, 33.

31. Baim, 8–9, 42.

32. Chasteen, 6.

33. http://www.jazzageclub.com/dancing/the-apache/ (accessed: June 2, 2010).

34. Giordano, 14–15.

35. Baim, 74.

36. Stephenson and Iaccarino, 29.

37. Carol Edrich, http://www.ballet.co.uk/magazines/yr_07/jul07/ce_waldorf _tango_tea_dance.htm (accessed: June 12, 2010).

38. Linda Tomko, *Dancing Class: Gender, Ethnicity, and Social Divides in American Dance, 1890–1920* (Bloomington and Indianapolis, IN: Indiana University Press, 1999), 23.

4

That Latin Beat: What They Did When They Got Here

It's a love affair between you and your partner and the music. You feel the music, you feel your partner, she feels you and she feels the music. So there the three of you are together. You've got a triangle, you know. Which one do you love best?

Frank Manning[1]

Continuing on the trail started in Chapter 3 of this three-way partnership of dancers with the music remains a central consideration in tracing what Latin social dances did when they got to the United States. Hardly a single major development in popular music went forward without some of that indispensably Latin "tinge." The Big Band Era of the 1930s to 1940s swept up Latin-influenced dances with it, such as swing, jive, lindy, and jitterbug. Then, following the revolution of the recording business and the popularity of mass-produced recorded music, dances such as the lambada and the hustle defined the Latin disco and dance club scene in the 1970s through 1980s. On the heels of disco, macarena and reggaeton evidenced a response to mass media, MTV video culture, and advertizing. An influx of Dominicans into the United States brought the national dances of the merengue and bachata, while bomba and plena also found new homes with Puerto Rican immigrants, especially in New York City.

Up until the communist takeover of the island, Cuban musicians had eagerly performed in the United States, touring everywhere and

Latin jazz musician Tito Puente and his all-star Latin jazz band entertain the crowd August 14, 1990, after Puente was honored with a star on the Hollywood Walk of Fame. (AP Photo/Kevork Djansezian.)

sometimes making their home in the United States. And they were as eagerly welcomed, since they provided the main push of creative flair in U.S. Latin music. But when the steady supply of fresh talent from Havana was interrupted by the fall of capitalism, U.S. musicians in the Latin mode—which included several African-Americans as well as Latinos—were left stranded. So, they experimented with a variety of possible fusions, with the predominant craze for rock and roll. The most well-known of these was boogaloo (or, bugalú), but variations included shing-a-ling and jala jala, among others.

Over time, this shifted toward greater sophistication in Latin jazz, the cool and the hot. An early "ultra-cool and smooth" Brazilian musical jazz style called bossa nova caught the ears of fans in the United States, but the dance that had been hastily invented by the dance studios to go with it never quite caught on. Finally, in the latter decades of the twentieth century, Latin jazz, soul, and related sounds became the expression of second-generation Latinos in the United

States, and the most popular of the Latin dance styles coalesced into one big, all-encompassing "sauce" called salsa.

By that time, Latin social dances were no longer exclusive to Spanish-speaking populations or African-Americans. Anyone could—and does—learn the steps, form, and style of Latin couples and line dances, either at the clubs or in guided group sessions at the new Latin dance studios, before heading out for a night of athletic dancing. And when it comes to a good workout, one of the most recent influences of Latin on the general culture is zumba exercise, which can be found in just about every health and fitness program anywhere in the United States—taken up by folks of all ages and abilities.

Big Band Dances with the Latin Tinge: Swing, Jive, Lindy, and Jitterbug

Where did folks go to dance to the big bands? Major cities like New York City, Chicago, Miami and Los Angeles were—and still are—known for their big ballrooms, usually attached to the larger hotels that supported a volume of tourist trade from all over the world. And that trade had a large appetite for the latest tropical Latin dances, since the tradition of an exotic good time went hand in hand with the clave beat. But virtually any tourist attraction site found it worth while to provide visitors with suitable dancing venues, including cruise ships, casinos, and theatres, in short, anywhere tourists were likely to hang out in the evenings for a drink, a little socializing, a floorshow, and—with little encouragement—an inclination to try out a new step or two.

Some 1940s and 1950s ballrooms were built to accommodate large groups of dancers who flocked for a good time to amusement parks. The ambitious Sea Lion Park at Coney Island, the first theme park to feature aquatic stunts and animals, tried to boost its appeal with a ballroom suited for a small army in 1899. Canobie Lake Park of Salem, New Hampshire, featured not only bowling alleys, a restaurant, swimming pool, ball park, and roller rink, but a ballroom. Hershey Park in Pennsylvania not only attracted golf pro Ben Hogan, but its ballroom housed the big band performances of Sammy Kaye, Guy Lombardo, Rudy Vallee, and Paul Whiteman. Idora not only features one of the best roller coasters in Ohio, but the largest ballroom between New York and Chicago, where as many as 2,500 couples at once could dance the night away in its 22,000 square feet of space. The Royal Terrace Ballroom of Peony Park features elegant gardens. Further West, the Trocodero Ballroom graces the Elitch's Gardens in Colorado, "an amusement park of distinction" that also supports cultured interests such as garden clubs and one of the oldest summer theatre seasons in the United States. The dance pavilion at the San Diego Belmont Amusement Park attracts square dancers every Friday night from hundreds of miles around.[2]

But tourists and vacationers weren't the only ones looking for large, open spaces in which to dance. The first big authentic Latin dance event in the United States was credited to New York City's East Harlem Puerto Rican civic association in 1930, when they rented the 110th Street and Fifth Avenue Golden Casino. In quick order, Latin music and staged dances filled other theatres and ballrooms. Also during the late 1930s, ballrooms were supported by a resurgence of prosperity for dance studios, nearly all of which offered instruction in the latest Latin styles.[3]

At the same time, African-American jook (juke) joints and honky-tonks all over the United States took in their share of dancers eager to lindy hop, jive, and jitterbug. During the 1930s and 1940s especially, these places offered cramped room for the improvisational athletics these dances encouraged. As is true of cramped space for the construction of buildings in big cities, if you can't spread out across the ground, then you must either go up or down. So up the dancers went—especially the girls, who were tossed, thrown, flipped or swung over the heads of their partners or rolled across their backs, while the boys dove for the floor in seemingly boneless backbends.[4]

Sometimes whites-only ballrooms would open a once-a-week dance for non-whites (for which both white and black bands might play in a single night to exchange musical styles), but in general there were few places where urban African-Americans could go to dance. At least in the ballrooms, there was more space for larger bands and a larger sound. And of these, the briefly-integrated Savoy of Harlem (which opened in 1926 but was closed in 1943 due to pressures against whites and blacks dancing together) offered a chance for Latin dancers and musicians to exchange styles with their mainstream counterparts— black and white—across the lindy, jive, and jitterbug.[5]

This Latin-influenced family of modern couples dancing became popular in the 1930s, hit a peak in post-World War II urban centers, and maintained a level of popularity ever since. They are true North-American-born social dances, blending Latin syncopations with African-American jazz and enthusiastic young dancers of every ethnic background. While the basics of these dances can be picked up from watching dancers in a club, they are also taught at dance studio franchises. Plenty of YouTube videos also demonstrate the steps, holds, moves, and rhythmic patterns; in fact, there's hardly a Latin dance of any kind that isn't available for basic instruction on YouTube, and these dances are no exception.

> Jive and Swing are pure [athletic] joy. In these steps, the dancers burst with exuberance at their youth, their skill, their beauty, their energy, and their spontaneous response to the power and drive of the music.[6]

As long-time dance studio favorites, these dances are favored by amateurs and professionals working to hone their skills for DanceSport competitions. Ballroom competition International Standard Latin Dance divisions include jive, while American Rhythm competitions include swing instead. These have more rules attached to them than social dance venues so that judges have a solid rubric upon which to evaluate the dancers: "As a Latin competition dance, jive requires dancers to hold a trained position and to move with precision. Feet point for kicks—very exaggerated movements. No lifts allowed."[7] But for exhibition performances and as vigorous social dances, swing, lindy, and the jitterbug do encourage considerable spontaneous innovation between partners, adding that sharp tinge of risk to some of the more daring routines couples can work out with each other while varying between closed and open holds. Swing especially has the kind of thrill effect of a carnival ride, in which partners set up both an in and out, as well as a circular momentum between them in what amounts to a figure eight locomotion on the floor, sort of a dancing that "doesn't go anywhere at the same time as it goes everywhere."[8]

Danced to a sharp 2/2 cut time and performed in a confined spot on the floor, these dances turn outrageous when pairs take turns showing off their fancy moves surrounded by a ring of other couples waiting their turn, just as for a mambo or rumba brava session. And almost any "hot" jazz music serves to support high athletic youthfulness as "the dancers are tossed, spun, twirled, and somersaulted to insistent rock and roll rhythms."[9] African-American roots mixed with a touch of Latin are proclaimed in the fancy dancing, which may have had the old-time minstrel show cakewalk and ragtime music as its grandparents. Large-scale dancing calls for a big sound and plenty of elbow and knee room.

Despite their quick leap into popularity, it took these dances a while to move from one area of the urban population into another. Jive and swing of the 1930s through 1950s were considered low-class dances in the United States, suited for jook joints and honky-tonks patronized by the poor, black, and "sexually-immoral," so "respectable" dancers avoided them at first. But as African-American rhythms gradually moved into the mainstream middle classes—speeded along by the music sales of vinyl records produced by the recording industry and dancing in the movies—teen dance parties imitated the good times shown in mass media variety dance programs such as *American Bandstand* (1952–1989).

Latin Dance Clubs and Disco

Several factors contributed to the end of the big bands and the dancing that they supported, union fights with the increasingly powerful recording industry and the rights to radio performances of the music among them. During the Depression and the advent of the radio as the primary source of inexpensive entertainment for most in the United States, big band music became the one sound Americans coast to coast and everywhere in between identified as their own. Advertizing and the movies were quick to pick up on the phenomenon, and big band music sold everything from cars to toothpaste.

While this venue for recording work remained open for musicians, the drain on live performances of all kinds (even the ballet) took a hit during World War II as vital touring was curtailed due to lack of transportation, and musicians went off to war. Even after the war and well into the 1960s, live band music and the Latin connection continued to wane, except for recording contracts and local school dances. Still, Latin and African-American musicians who served in the war continued their exchanges of musical styles, and dancers continued to trade snappy step routines in the dances. But in the mainstream United States social dancing, rock and roll was king, and only whites were shown dancing together in the media. And it seemed likely that things would stay that way, until the previously docile "baby boomers" suddenly seemed to turn society upside-down.

Enter the world of disco (short for discothèque, or club) dancing, which continued to widen the door to exchanges among white, black, and Latin music and dance styles. This venue was supported by women and the GLBT (gay, lesbian, bisexual, and transgender) communities of large cities across the United States as part of the cultural revolution (civil rights, anti-Viet Nam war, women's equality, Rainbow Coalition, etc.). The new freedoms were not simply spoken. They were made into action, and some of that action spilled over in freestyle modes on the disco dance floor:

> By 1977, more than fifteen thousand discos were operating throughout the United States; by the end of the decade, discos like Tramps and "2001" were franchised; most large motels and hotels across the country ran discos in their basements.[10]

Disco may have gotten its start from New York City apartment dances as a reaction against the commercialization and overpowering influence of steady 1950s and 1960s rock and roll music. If so, it kept some of that more intimate appeal, as disco dancing takes place in much smaller venues than ballrooms; only thirty to a hundred or so dancers fit snuggly into a disco club space. It's also not very well lighted, giving license to lambada and the hustle "dirty dancing" moves between couples.

Disco is so-called because the music is "on disc"; that is, recorded instead of live. A DJ (disc jockey) displaces the band leader with arrangements of continuous sounds (as well as visual effects in lighting) electronically-arranged in such a way that Latin, soul, jazz, and other music are linked together in a continuous thread. Disco sound is difficult to describe, but "thick," "lush," and "layered" are words that come to mind, having borrowed from 1960s to 1970s psychedelia. Disco dancers lose themselves in the artificial environment, leaving the miseries of the ordinary world outside, making disco a creation of a kind of baby-boomer fantasy, with a pair of dancers in the center of the floor.

The disco beat is described as "four on the floor"; a kind of marching drive not unlike merengue, with its 4/4 pounding of the bass drum pedal. In time, disco wore out its glitzy high-tech novelty, and has more or less gone the way of big hair and bell bottoms. But in recent years disco has begun to make something of a comeback in a revised and updated form, a novelty to those too young to have remembered the original. Regardless of where it goes from here, disco has done a great deal toward the development of Latin freestyle dancing.

Hustle

The word "hustle" actually stems from the Dutch word for "shake"; in underworld lingo, a hustler was one who shook up or jostled a victim while his confidante picked the victim's pocket.[11] But watching a couple dance the hustle, there's some question as to who might be hustling whom. Hustle is the quintessential disco dance, well suited to the general disco club fantasy under revolving mirror balls and a seemingly endless stream of music. Many variations and names include "Latin hustle," "lindy hustle," "American hustle," "tango hustle," "three-count hustle" or "street hustle." But no matter its description, any hustle was part of the return to close-couples dancing after the freedom–loving, individual, idiosyncratic dances of the late 1960s had faded and people were looking for a new way to dance together as couples again.

The holds in Latin hustle are very close and full-bodied, with plenty of swing alternated with snap turns, kicks, lunges, and dips. Both partners strut their stuff, though some degree of machismo gives the male partner a little more opportunity to display his dancing skills. Hustle dancers start off with a closed-couple hold. Then, the push and pull momentum of the dancers' turning movements gradually spin outward from their spot center on the dance floor, as the lady spins away from and into her partner's arms.[12] The hustle is listed in this chapter as a Latin-influenced social dance that got its start around 1970 in urban Black and Puerto Rican bars of New York City. Alternatively—perhaps simultaneously—the dance is also credited to Cubans coming into Miami, who mixed swing with salsa and fitted it to disco dancing.[13] One way or the other, the hustle is a note or two romantically softer than jive, swing, or lindy, to which it is sometimes compared.

While the New York version of the Latin hustle is slower, with more footwork and rotated spot tracking in place, the Los Angeles hustle is faster, with fewer rotating moves. Overall, the hustle ranges in difficulty and has been well-commercialized by dance studios offering to teach it. But despite its popularity generated from such movies as *Saturday Night Fever* (1977), aerials and trick dancing took the hustle out of reach for most casual social dancers. Besides, the Texas two-step and country and western offered some of the same feel without as much practice to get going.[14] Still, Travolta parodies continue to pop up from time to time in film, notably in *Short Circuit I* (1986), and Pixair's 2010 summer hit, *Despicable Me*.

Lambada

The very briefly-popular Brazilian "dirty dancing" style called the lambada showed up in the United States early in the 1990s as part of a resurgence of interest in Caribbean music, and owes much of its revised style to merengue/salsa. Lambada (which perhaps comes from the Bahian word meaning "strong hit," or "strike") moves from one side to the other instead of swinging front to back, a feature that, as the lady wears a tight skirt slit high up the side of the thigh, teases the possibility of seeing more than is decent in public. The dance music was brought into the United States by a couple of French entrepreneurs from Brazil, who evidently bought the rights to more than 300 tunes that had been playing on local radio stations. Dance studios in the United States kept it going for a while as the latest dance out of South America, even though the Bahian origins of the music were considered low-class in Brazil.[15] It is also said to be something of a combination of zouk, reggaeton, and maxixie, with a dash of calypso music to steam it up. However, it would be very difficult to see any of these specifically in a lambada, which does have some striking dynamics as it goes back and forth between very slow and sensual to quick, jazzy moves.

Lambada is performed to a pretty fast 4/4 tempo, with three steps followed by a pause. But its real notoriety lies in its very close hold with pelvic grinds and thigh-locks, which middle-aged baby-boomers found to be very spicy indeed, at least for a while. However, their children had already engaged in this kind of dancing before the lambada came along, so they were not particularly impressed, and more or less ignored it.[16]

Macarena

While conga lines occasionally still form at lawn parties and celebrations, the "hokey-pokey" fun of a macarena may erupt sporadically at restaurants serving Mexican dishes and margaritas even today. At its peak, macarena made it into the movies—notably the 2001 Disney film *Shrek*—and participants chanted their way through the dance at both

Republican and Democratic Party conventions of 1996. However, interest in this dance as a mainstay of Latin social dancing has not endured, perhaps because it is so closely-attached to a single pop-hit recording. Line dancing has always been fun to do at parties or large gatherings of any kind, and the macarena has a good combination of repetition and changes of direction as each dancer adds to the movements in his or her own style to make it interesting. The dance apparently first spread from California to Florida and New York City around 1993 with a 1960s Cuban beat. But almost as soon as it appeared, the craze also vanished. And a recent attempt to promote a new version of the macarena called the tongoneo as a marketing tool for Miller Lite beer hasn't quite yet made the big time, either:

> The Mexico City group Mestizzo famous for their version of the song *La Macarena*, has joined forces with Miller Lite to launch the Miller Tongoneo. The Mexican group is featured in a new Miller commercial, and they are visiting Texas to promote the tongoneo.[17]

Reggaeton

If you tell the kids not to put beans in their ears, they are sure to give it a try precisely because you said not to do it. Reggaeton is just the sort of dance that conscientious parents would want to keep their daughters well away from, and that very fact, it seems, lends it the fascination of forbidden pleasure. It is not uncommon for young girls hooked on the dance to sneak out their skimpy reggaeton outfits in baggy purses as they leave the house so they can change out of their more conservative street clothes when they get to the dance. Once there, the girls compete with one another in the most outrageous displays of sexual dance moves they can think up.

As a relative newcomer to the group of Latin social dances, reggaeton grew out of a combination of popular Jamaican reggae music mixed with Spanish rap, the first productions of which appeared in 1994 in the NYC clubs Playero 37 and The Noise. The rapper was accompanied by reggae beats as the edgy words were improvised in Spanish. Pretty soon, dancers in small groups as well as couples started to move to the sound in an improvisational manner, and the dance firmed up as a thoroughly urban dance club style, the sole purpose of which seems to be to push a thin line between social dancing and exhibitionist "pornography." Part of the youth hip-hop club scene, the dance is an up-tempo reggae sound coming from reggaemuffin and Miami hip-hop, a style influenced by other Latin dances like bomba and salsa.

One form is a "booty shaking" competition among two or three girls dancing close together on a raised platform, for which the girls receive rapt attention and verbal encouragement from all the males present. As a couples' dance it encourages the most explicitly-sexual moves as a response to the enthusiastic urging of onlookers. While not exactly a disco phenomenon, reggaeton dancers participate in small group crowds tightly-packed into the small space of a dance club under dim lighting, suggesting the freedom to "move as you choose" without censorship. One popular type of reggaeton is called "perreo," in which "a couple in the middle of the dance floor is surrounded by other dancers [who encourage them to] imitate dogs' sexual act."[18] Whether vulgar or exciting (depending upon your point of view), reggaeton offers a freedom of movement and an escape from the ordinary of life experience.

Dominican Nationalism: Bachata and Merengue

This snappy pair of dances originated in the Dominican Republic, and although merengue is probably the more well-known of the two outside of Caribbean dance floors, bachata has recently come into its own. Traditionally, both musical song styles included social commentary connected to a distinctively Dominican Latin identity wherever they were performed. Hot spots for bachata and merengue dancing in the United States thrive wherever Dominicans gather—mostly in Miami or New York City, though it has spread to Los Angeles, Seattle, and Chicago. However, almost any Latin social dance event anywhere in the United States is likely to include one or the other, and often both.

They complement each other and are very close in style, with attractive variations of tightly-closed torso-to-torso holds and open positions between partners. The steps bear the same marching relationship to the rhythmic patterns of the music. Tempo for merengue is usually a little faster. Performed to a very fast 2/4 tempo, the step is a march per beat, and with four punching knees, it takes some skill for a pair of merengue dancers to work together. Bachata step is also very simple (step to the side, close, step to the side, touch). However, the man has the best opportunity to demonstrate his classy moves while the lady tends to hold down the base rhythmic pattern from which he departs and returns.

A textural variation between a smooth upper body carriage over a contrasting rolling sway in the lower body, Latin motion achieved through a relaxed knee action, transferring the weight from one side to the other, is another feature shared between merengue and bachata. But while merengue has this sway in each march step for both partners, the Latin motion of a bachata is emphasized most in the hips of the lady (in high heels, of course). She uses the fourth count of the basic bachata step-together-step-touch pattern to press her hip up on the touch of her toe quickly (with a slight pause) before she rolls it down into the next step, which is the first step to the side, back (or forward) on the next bar of the music.

A suave style is key to classy execution of a merengue especially; bachata is a little more relaxed. Hands and elbows are held high while the upper body generally "floats" above the movements of hips, knees, and legs. A lateral "slide" of the ribcage in the direction the steps take makes a kind of bridge between the strictly quiet shoulders and the movements of hips, legs, and feet. Partner holds for these dances also allow for quite a bit of variation, although bachata turns and holds resemble swing and lindy hop.

Depending on the venue, men generally wear informal street clothes and tennis shoes. Ladies may be similarly informal in their clothing, but these dances require heels to really accentuate "the swing in the backyard" effect. Depending on how intimate they wish to be, bachata and merengue dancers may choose to hold each other tightly torso to torso, or barely connect by the hands; however, hand contact between partners is rarely broken over the course of the dance. While merengue partners stick to a spot on the dance floor, bachata partners may choose to move or spot, often swinging each other across a closed figure eight pattern, again much as in swing or lindy.

These similarities between bachata and merengue make it easy to shift from one to the other in a single dance, which often happens in contemporary dance parties and Latin dance clubs. The usual inclination is to dance bachata steps during the vocal section, then move on to the faster march of a merengue during the midsection instrumental interlude. Even so, they are different dances.

Bachata gets its name from the trio of musical instruments that traditionally accompany the song/dance; the guitar is prominent, supported by bongos and maracas in 2/4 cut or 4/4 time. With its sharp kicks between partners' legs and an extremely tight, undulating torso-to-torso hold between partners, bachata can be performed as a very sexy exhibition dance resembling a maxixie, tango, or lambada. The close hold is broken only for tight turns, or in order to execute a slow swing-dip. Alternatively for dancers not desiring such full-body contact, bachata may be danced with all varieties of open holds, according to skill. As in a maxixie or tango, bachata dancers can include knee-snaps between—or even around—their partner's legs. On the touch beat in the step pattern, the toe may describe an arc on the floor to one side or the other of the partner's position. The man may also touch his foot forward or backward in a flat-footed lift and drop arc, (sometimes even reaching to touch his hand to his lifted foot) adding to the sensual suggestiveness of the dance.[19]

Old-time Dominican bachata dances were accompanied by salty song lyrics that served an intensely-exaggerated machismo point of view. They were sung by men about masculine pleasure in abundant food, drink, and the mysterious powers of women to control and deceive. The mix of bawdy humor and lamentation limited the original bachata in the Dominican Republic to late-night all-male venues such as bars and colmados, to which respectable women and families were not welcome.[20] Women of questionable reputation, however, were much in demand.

How the name merengue stuck to the dance is not entirely clear. "The first mention of merengue occurs around the 1850s, when the Dominicans overthrew the occupying Haitians and took their independence from Spain.[21] One possible origin of the name is that the dance resembles the action of an egg-beater necessary to whip up the frothy confection of sugar and egg-whites topping for a pie.[22] This reliable action is best accomplished with a flexible knee, which requires partners to be slightly off-center to one another so their knees can freely move without hitting each other.

Traditional accompaniment for merengue includes a button accordion, güiro, marimbula, and tambora drum, but a contemporary merengue band may include just about any modern instrumental arrangement, including electric guitar. Merengue is also danced in the next-door country, Haiti.

As one of the easiest of all Latin dances for couples to learn in very short order, merengue can be casually picked up at any dance event and danced with a "proper" space between pairs. As well as being a quick and easy dance to learn to perform adequately well, it is also highly adaptable to a wide variety of body types and stylistic preferences of the dancers. But mastering its style takes practice to perfect in a tightly closed, full-body hold because two very opposite kinds of things are going on—above the waist and below. Its cool upper-body carriage bespoke of what in the Dominican Republic is referred to as "criollo," or a high-class item from Spain rather than something low-class and home-made.

The distinction is more racial than national, however; for although certain in its Afro-Caribbean origins, the merengue dance had somehow got the criollo label, and it was vigorously promoted as "the" Dominican national dance during the regime of Trujillo (1891–1961). If Trujillo said everybody had to dance the merengue, then everybody danced the merengue, for so feared was he by Dominicans that it was said that even a glance from him had the power to kill someone from across the street. Eager to establish The Dominican Republic as a Euro-sophisticated spot in the Caribbean, Trujillo attempted to eradicate as many traces of Afro-Dominican heritage from the country as possible, and somehow the merengue dance fit the bill.[23]

In addition to continuing as a popular Latin dance for all social occasions, merengue is sometimes added to the American Rhythm section of the Latin Dances in DanceSport competitions. Bachata, on the other hand, is ideally-suited for zumba exercise routines, although both bachata and merengue constitute good cardio-workouts for enthusiasts. Despite its exhibition potential, bachata is not part of the ballroom DanceSport competition series. It is sometimes taught in dance studios as a rather tame social dance (described by some as "like a bolero") or as a practice dance for competition pairs working on developing their skills in other Latin dance styles.[24]

Puerto Rican Nationalism: Bomba and Plena

Bomba most commonly refers to a dance, while plena is very much like a Cuban son, a social commentary song and music style that may, or may not, have dancing with it. Traditionally distinct, it is not unusual in modern references to conflate these two terms together; a quick view of YouTube videos online show any number of "bomba y plena" dances. A relative newcomer to the tropical Latin dance club scene in the United States, bomba started out as a clever, energetic West African slave import to its New World home in the coastal plantations of Puerto Rico. It is sometimes referred to as "Puerto Rico's equivalent of the rumba brava."[25] Puerto Ricans came into the United States because the 1917 Jones Act made Puerto Rico a commonwealth of the United States, and Puerto Ricans were granted citizenship. Many settled in Spanish Harlem. Another wave of Puerto Ricans arrived in the1930s as a result of being "driven from Puerto Rico both by the Depression and by the destruction of small-scale farming through the development of intensive, single-crop agriculture (sugar, coffee and tobacco)."[26]

As a traditional folk dance, bomba pairs dancers in several promenade open holds, and the entrance of the dance couples in this opening promenade clearly announces "Puerto Rico is here!" Holding inside hands (the gentleman on the right with the lady on the left) and progressing side-by-side forward and back is another bomba figure, one of several that reflect a European dance (such as contras or minuets) overlay. Since bomba moves don't allow for much in the way of closed holds, the man may take the waist of the lady while her hands are busy waving the flounces of her skirt.

But plantation slave dances are what give bomba its distinctive flavor. Dancers are barefooted, and the placement of the foot calls to mind a soft, sandy ground rather than hard, indoor flooring. Shines front and back allow the dancers shimmies and torso rolls. There is always a lot of flirting going on, upon which the audience, musicians, and singers may offer helpful encouragement. But the relationship between the pair is not always in accord as they eye each other in the way of challenging birds. Some of the same sense of competition and challenge is also present in modern day bombas, particularly when same-gender pairs dance together.[27]

There are also plenty of gestures and movements in which both dancers can display mastery of isolation; that is, as one part of the body is following one rhythmic sequence, a different part is independently following another rhythm. While the man waves his straw hat or takes a kerchief from the lady and waves it, he bends toward the ground, high-stepping and executing a pivot or "dart" turn (that is, with one foot planted at the center of his turn while the other foot darts from that center to the perimeter of the circle). For her part, the lady is dressed in full, flowing skirts which she holds out in both hands. As she dances, she flounces her skirts, shaking and swirling the ruffles in a way that brings to mind Mexican folk dances. The lady also kneels on the ground, and there is considerable polyrhythmic motion in her shoulders, torso, and hips.

Plena music stands on its own with a root folk tradition in Puerto Rico, growing up among the slave population, though its urban form appeared during World War I among the lower labor classes. Songs imported from Barbados, seasoned by Spanish romances, also contributed to plena lyrics and melodic patterns. Heavy on the driving rhythm of a 2/4 or 6/8 percussion at a brisk pace, plena music features an accordion or guitar, several panderos, and an assortment of shakers and scrapers like a güiro. Later, and in its commercial form, horns, congas, and timbales amplified the sound. Saucy improvisation has always been important to plena music; the Puerto Rican showman drummer known as Bumbún was expert at "rolling his instrument across his shoulders, over his head or along the floor, without losing the beat."[28]

The plena song is as important as its rhythm, and the main vocalist (a woman called the "laina") is its driving force. She repeats a short melodic phrase that is answered by the chorus, or sometimes the dancers themselves. Topics in the lyrics of the song vary, but usually pertain to the pressures of impoverished urban life. There is considerable exchange between musicians and dancers, as dancers may, during an improvisation sequence, face the drummers while spectators add their own clapping; Dancers take turns challenging the drums, creating a dialogue with their movements that the solo drummer answers in a call-and-response pattern with a lead singer and a chorus. The words are traditional and improvisatory, often revolving around events in the community.[29]

Bomba is a great deal of fun just as a mass dance without partners. With a step on every beat of the lengthy music set, even one dance is a complete cardio-workout, and bomba figures do sometimes show up in zumba exercise routines. The little hopping "scoot" or "chug" (forward-back or side-to-side) in bomba is best accomplished without shoes; socks on a smooth floor give the optimum effect in evoking bare feet against sand.

New York City is the most likely place to find spontaneous bomba y plena events in the United States, instigated by Puerto Rican immigrants yet open to anyone who wants to join—especially at Central Park or on barrio streets. Even as enjoyed by couples and line groups of dancers in Latin dance clubs around the United States, bomba retains strong ties to its African roots. However, modern social bomba dancers don't usually sport plantation costumes, favoring comfortable street clothing instead.

Latin Jazz: Bossa Nova and Salsa

Latin jazz doesn't often get much mention in the history of music in the United States, but it's still there all the same, and a good ear can find it in any number of unlikely spots. Duke Ellington's 1931 *It Don't Mean a Thing (If It Ain't Got That Swing)*, and his 1941 *Moon over Cuba* are a couple of examples. Harlem's Savoy Ballroom drummer, Chick Webb, knew how to set a Latin twinge to his beat to keep the dancers going, and Puerto Rican pianist Noro Morales provided an upscale Latin sheen to the American music he played at the Stork Club. In 1947, big-band leader Stan Kenton got "Mister Bongo" (Jack Costanzo) to play in an arrangement of *Peanut Vendor* with him, which sparked a Latin dance craze around the world.[30] About the same time, Dizzy Gillespie collaborated with rumba drummer Chano Pozo for a foray into "cubop."

Even in the very origins of jazz in the United States, the Latin clave beat was indispensible, if unacknowledged. "Ragtime pianist Jelly Roll Morton linked the twin ports of Havana and New Orleans when he described jazz as possessing a 'Spanish tinge.'"[31] The closed-hold partnership continued to develop through the 1940s, when Army service brought Afro-American and Latin music lovers together. Even after the war, it seemed natural for them to collaborate, and the result was so stunning that social dancers didn't want to miss out on any of it.

At about the same time, Cuban orchestras manned by Puerto Ricans were also experimenting with the sound potential of big-band American jazz. Improvisation paved the way for Afro-Cuban and Afro-American sounds to continue trying out different kinds of melds; Manchito's band hit it big at the Palladium, and along with Tito Puente and Tito Rodrígues (who often held drumming playoffs to the delight of the crowd), he became one of the three "Mambo Kings" of the Palladium ballroom. "Mongo Santamaría, who originally worked with Tito Puente, became one of the most widely-known Latin musicians in jazz, and also struck gold with Latin versions of American songs" (e.g., *Watermelon Man* by Herbie Hancock).[32]

Generally, Cuban arrangements set the trends, though most musicians playing them were Puerto Rican, with a few Dominicans. Cuban and Puerto Rican horn players also found work in jazz bands and in the orchestra pit of Broadway musicals. The talented Alberto Socarras not only played his group as a Cotton Club warm-up, but also cut recordings of rumbas and boleros, and hired trumpeter Dizzy Gillespie for an American note or two in his Latin sound.[33] The three-way phenomenon of two dancers and the music has never found a more exciting, ever-changing frame on the social dance floor. The pace was set, and while many Latin dances ran right into salsa, others left their traces as they fell by the wayside.

Bossa Nova

Slang for "new beat," bossa nova is a cut 4/4 time at moderate tempo and is truly a modern metropolitan social dance hybrid, the music for which fuses one style of Brazilian samba with the sleek sophistication of modern jazz. Something of a late-comer to the United States compared with other Latin dances like the tango or rumba, bossa nova never became a popular dance on the social dance floor, and is not set for exhibition or DanceSport competition. Nevertheless, the dance is flexible to many interesting steps and figures, and is easy to learn.[34]

The dance really came about because of the music, which was first played in the cafés of Rio de Janeiro in 1958. In a bid to bring this "new Brazilian jazz" music into the United States, Audio-Fidelity music records President-Producer Sidney Frey scouted Rio for bossa nova musicians who could perform in a concert at Carnegie Hall in 1962. According to bossa nova enthusiast Steven Byrd (on his website), the concert won over the attending audience to this new jazz style, and some of the artists remained in the United States to quickly capitalize on this popularity:

> The classic Getz/Gilberto (with Jobim on piano) was recorded in just two days on March 18 and 19, 1963 including the first bilingual version of *The Girl from Ipanema* by Gilberto's wife Astrud singing the English lyrics.[35]

As a true Latin jazz hybrid, bossa nova combines movement qualities characteristic of both Spanish and tropical Latin dances. The gentle, smoothly-flowing partnering brings it into comparison with the Spanish Latin dances as it both moves across the floor and stays closed in one spot, according to the particular step being performed. As in the Spanish Latin Dances, bossa nova maintains quiet shoulders and a flat-footed contact with the floor, while the holds, figures, and arms (held gentle-elbowed with palms facing down) evoke a folk dance, contra dance, or minuet stance. Even though the basic step (slow, quick, quick) reflects the romantic tensions of a bolero, bossa nova forgoes serious sensual intensity in favor of a far more relaxed and easy-going pleasure.

At the same time, the short, aligned steps, close footwork, and subdued Latin motion (more of a rocking motion than a saucy "flip of the hip," especially as taught in dance studios) connect bossa nova to other tropical Latin dances. Some instructors have described the bossa nova as a sort of a "reverse American rumba" pattern. The dance also features a flexible knee action for both partners, but the point of the dance is a smooth, cool, and self-reserved appearance.

Bossa nova music has been far more popular in the general public than its dance, and is also a hybrid between a distinctly urban and sophisticated cool jazz style and Latin "heat." It is hard to understand why the bossa nova dance never quite became as popular as its music, but the fact that the music didn't originally have a dance to go with it led to some rather hasty marketing of a suitable couples' dance by both the Astaire and Arthur Murray studios in an effort to boost record album sales. But although some liked the dance, most found the pastiche of samba/mambo moves with a bit of the twist thrown in—despite catchy dance move descriptions like the "knee-knock" or "peeling the banana"—"too fast for a slow dance and too slow for a fast dance."[36]

The music, however, continued to intrigue, with its sleek vocals and percussion mix. Of these the agogô bells are most closely associated with 1960s bossa nova music in the United States and Brazil. These are a set of two or three conical-shaped bells of different sizes that are played much like a cowbell in Brazilian music, as they are struck by a metal mallet. A more versatile accompaniment than the cowbell, the modern version of the instrument yields a "brighter" tone. Contemporary agogôs have the bells connected to each other by a handle or they are mounted on a stand, tuned to each other at a minor third or sometimes to a second. They are made of 18-gauge steel and relatively pitched a minor third apart. A wonderfully-patterned counter rhythm to the base beat of drums similar to tamborims can be achieved with this instrument.

Although it never quite caught on in the United States outside of dance studios as a charming couples dance, bossa nova has recently gained a new following as a line dance in which the footwork makes a constant change of direction, where it also makes a nice transition sequence in a zumba exercise routine.

Salsa

While bossa nova music made inroads in mainstream awareness of the dance potential of the Latin jazz beat in the United States, it would take an entirely different kind of fusion of dance styles to kick it firmly onto the social dance floor in a big way. Enter the enduringly-popular Cuban-based tropical Latin dance of salsa, at home on any social dance floor and sometimes performed as an exciting exhibition dance. Since its first appearance in the United States, salsa has steadily grown to be so popular worldwide that it has virtually become synonymous with the essential Latin Dance club scene. The origin of the term "salsa" is pretty clear, referring to a food condiment that is a rich mix of textures and colors with spicy, tart, and bland flavors, each of which is distinct and yet they all go well together. And there must be hundreds—if not thousands—of variations of salsa served with Latin dishes. Although the comparison of dance and music to food wrinkles the noses of some, the name has stuck: "The name salsa dates only from the 1960s, but salsa's dance moves draw on a centuries-old tradition."[37]

The first conscious connection between the music and the food may have been made in 1966, when a Venezuelan music radio show described the contemporary Cuban music it broadcast as "La hora del sabor, la salsa y el bembe" (loosely translated as "the hour of flavor, spiciness, and blessings"), or music for body and soul. But it took a boost from the recording industry to bring it forward, when "By the end of the 1970s the word [salsa] was synonymous with the sound of Latin New York, as created by Fania Records Latin New York's take on Cuban dance music, played mostly by Puerto Rican musicians."[38]

Fast, sassy, and jazzy, salsa is a true urban-born "hybrid" of African, Latin, and European social dances without clear connections to any particular foundational folk or country style. In fact, salsa claims many parents, among them rhythm and blues with Afro-Cuban conjunto/jazz.[39] The music caught on with mostly Puerto Rican musicians, and

Celia Cruz accepts her award for best salsa album during the 3rd Annual Latin Grammy Awards Wednesday, September 18, 2002, in the Hollywood district of Los Angeles. (AP Photo/Kevork Djansezian.)

was melded in with their own experimentation with son. This Latin jazz music became synonymous with the "Nuyorican salsa" sound and dance style, which pepped up its international urban beat with electric keyboards and other modern musical instruments. Other, more traditional instruments underwent an overhaul; 1960s salsa cowbells got additional notes out of the percussion instrument by being cut with grooves across the surface. The bells have become a hallmark of Puerto Rican salsas ever since.[40] Puerto Rican salsa music also gets a kick in the horn sections from swing bands, because during World War II and immediately after, radio music featured the big band sounds of Glenn Miller and Count Basie.[41]

But Latin jazz in its own form took a leap forward when, in 1971, Fania production artists put on a show at the Cheetah Club in Manhattan, which was filmed as *Nuestra Cosa Latina*, or "Our Latin Thing." In 1973 they performed at Yankee Stadium for 20,000 people. Johnny Pacheco conducted, Celia Cruz rendered twenty minutes of improvisation on her hit song *Bemba colorá*, and Ray Baretto and Mongo Santamariá were up for a dueling conga fit to curl your toes. And it wasn't just all Latin either; jazz, rock and roll, and African-style music fit in, too. This historic concert was filmed to be released in 1974, along with a two-album record set, *Fania All Stars Live at Yankee Stadium*. Oh, and the name of the film? *Salsa*. Pretty soon, Fania's bands were touring all over the world with the new sound, and a new/old dance for couples, for lines, and for individual dancers was filling the Latin social dance floors along with it.

Today, salsa—like the tango—is more a style of dancing to a wide variety of musical sounds than a dance closely-associated with a particular kind of music. But just as Latin jazz suggests a fusion of common elements gleaned from separate Latin sources, so too does salsa combine elements of different Latin dances, whether Cuban, Puerto Rican, Dominican, or Brazilian. Salsa kept changing, which also meant that it kept growing. In the 1980s, it turned distinctly romantic (salsa romántica), of which the song *Noches Calientes* (Hot Nights) sold close to half a million copies. The late 1980s brought on another transformation into what was called "salsa erotica," for which the male dancer concentrated on his pelvic gyrations to explicitly sexual lyrics set to a kind of repetitive—well, probably it was meant to be seductive—music. There followed all kinds of experimental crossovers with hip-hop, salsa/reggae, electro-salsa, salsa-rock, and salsa/merengue (more than half a million Dominicans surged into New York City around 1988), as well as a brief period in which flamenco hand claps and guitars got into a merengue/hip-hop version. This trait of continual readaptation made it possible for musicians to transition from one long-term era right into the next without missing a beat, as "The honorable King of Latin Jazz, Tito Puente, with over a half a century of crackling timbales solos, continues to produce music for the latest generation."[42]

If Tito Puente is the King of Latin Jazz, then the Queen of Salsa must certainly be Celia Cruz. Gifted with a full-bodied operatic vocal range, Cruz excelled in split-second scats, rapier-sharp humor, and timing in her improvisations, and presented an unforgettable image as she danced and sang in sequined outfits that took her costumers weeks to make. Her repertoire was astonishingly versatile; from tributes to Afro-Cuban saints, to salsa raps, Latin ballads, and American salsa.[43]

In Miami dance clubs today, it would seem there is almost no other Latin dance than salsa, and nearly every dance studio offers lessons in the latest version of "Salsa On2" or "Nightclub Style," for which partners seldom lose handhold throughout flashy spins of the ladies, or cross-shoulder passes that make this version of salsa look very much like a swing dance set to a Latin syncopation percussive beat. And if someone shows up without a date, well, "Salsa On1" fits right in with the same music. If a couple wants to merengue/salsa, they just keep marching throughout next to a Colombian cumbia couple, while the timbale changes rhythm for a Cuban salsa and the dancers fall right in.[44] What the future can be for salsa is hard to say, but if it keeps changing with the times and with the variations of relevancy it has shown so far, perhaps with a "mosaic of salsa, reggae, rap, and house"[45] there is no end in sight, and the Latin beat just goes on.

Let's Zumba: Dance Exercise

Given its athletic step-per-beat nature, it shouldn't be much of a surprise that Latin dance has even found its way into fitness programs. Enter zumba, a generic mix of mambo, cha-cha, samba, and salsa steps and figures set to variably-paced tropical Latin music. As interest in other fitness fads like kickboxing and step classes across the United States waned, zumba exercise cashed in on the popularity of such TV shows as *Dancing With the Stars*.[46] As of 2008, zumba ranked among the most sought-after fitness activities in the United States for hour-long cardio-workouts.

Zumba (now a brand name; the official Zumba® website states that the name is based on a Colombian slang word meaning to "move fast and have fun") was first introduced in the late 1990s by contemporary Colombian dancer and choreographer Alberto "Beto" Perez. As he reports on his website, Perez, who was teaching aerobics classes in Colombia, forgot his fitness tape one day and decided to substitute some salsa and merengue music. Fitting Latin dance moves to the music, Perez found that his students were delighted with the change. He brought his new fitness dance to Miami in 2001. There, Perez eventually joined forces with Alberto Perlman, co-founder and CEO of Zumba Fitness to franchise zumba internationally.[47]

Today, zumba continues to be one of the most popular exercise classes across the United States, and even in small towns, fitness and wellness clubs offer zumba sessions to enthusiasts of all ages as often as twice a day. Zumba is performed by individuals following the moves of the instructor just as they would for an aerobics class. The footwork in this dance exercise activity is similar to step-exercise, as

Personal trainer Janel Gauger, 28, of Irvine, Calif., teaches people to dance off the pounds with Zumba, moving to music with a Latin beat. (AP Photo/Chelsea J. Carter.)

steps forward, back, and side-to-side V's and grapevine patterns alternate with changes of direction. But there the similarity to routine exercise sessions ends. A really good zumba session depends upon the skill of its choreography to move participants in all directions and exercise the whole body. And the music helps everyone forget that they are exercising via the enjoyment of the dance, which provides periods of variations in the pace of the workout that ease fatigue without actually having to stop moving.

Notes

1. Frank Manning [a member of Whitey's Lindy Hoppers in 1935 at the Savoy] from: Gerald Jonas, *Dancing: the Pleasure, Power, and Art of Movement* (New York: Harry N. Abrams, Inc., 1998), 179–181.

2. Al Griffin, *"Step Right Up, Folks!"* (Chicago, IL: Henry Regnery Company, 1974).

3. Ralph G. Giordano, *Social Dancing in America: Lindy Hop to Hip Hop, 1901–2000*, Vol. 2 (Westport, CN and London: Greenwood Press, 2007), 66–67.

4. Katarina Hazzard-Gordon, *Jookin': The Rise of Social Dance Formations in African-American Culture* (Philadelphia, PA: Temple University Press, 1990), 126–127.

5. http://www.swingmusic.net/getready.html (accessed: March 12, 2010).

6. John Lawrence Reynolds, *Ballroom Dancing: The Romance, Rhythm and Style* (San Diego, CA: Laurel Glen Publishing, 1998), 43–44.

7 Yvonne Marceau, "Ballroom Dance Competition," In Selma Jeanne Cohen, Ed. *International Encyclopedia of Dance*, Vol. 1 (New York: Oxford University Press, 1999), 359.

8. Author's unpublished journal notes, August, 2000.

9. Reynolds, 22.

10. Sally Sommer, "Twentieth-Century Social Dance since 1980," In Selma Jeanne Cohen, Ed. *International Encyclopedia of Dance*, Vol. 5 (New York: Oxford University Press, 1999), 163–636.

11. Richard M. Stephenson and Joseph Iaccarino, *The Complete Book of Ballroom Dancing* (Garden City, NY: Doubleday & Company, Inc., 1980), 53.

12. Sommer, 163–636.

13. Sonny Watson's Streetswing.com Archives streetswing.com/histmain/d5index. (accessed: August 8, 2009).

14. Sonny Watson's Streetswing.com Archives streetswing.com/histmain/d5index. (accessed: August 8, 2009).

15. http://www.latinnet.co.uk/History/Lambada.htm (accessed: June 12, 2010).

16. Sommer, pp. 163–636.

17. Raul S. Llamas, "Mestizzo and Tongoneo Electrifies San Antonio," In *La Prensa de San* Antonio, August 4, 1996, (accessed: March 5, 2010).

18. http://www.reggaeton-in-cuba.com/en/history-cont.htm (accessed: February 20, 2010).

19. http://www.youtube.com/user/rasman1978 (accessed: May 11, 2010).

20. http://www.starlightdancestudio.com/Dance_Styles.html (accessed: July 7, 2008).

21. Steward, 107.

22. Lori Heikkila, http://www.centralhome.com/ballroomcountry/merengue.htm (accessed: May 10, 2010).

23. Author's unpublished journal notes, September 18, 1982.

24. http://www.kokoloco.com.au/styles.htm (accessed: July 15, 2008).

25. Isabelle Leymarie, *Cuban Fire: the Saga of Salsa and Latin Jazz* (London and New York: Continuum, 2002), 99.

26. Steward, 47.

27. http://www.youtube.com/watch?v=MzyBT5da5Do (accessed: May 20, 2010).

28. Steward, 96.

29. Anuradha Muralidharan, *Bomba* (Feb 6, 2007), In http://worlddance.suite101.com/article.cfm/bomba#ixzz0fnTEsr0L (accessed: May 7, 2010).

30. Steward, 49.

31. Seward, 148.

32. Steward, 151.

33. Steward, 50.

34. Stephenson and Iaccarino, 47–48.

35. http://www.brazzil.com/p122mar03.htm (accessed: August 9, 2009).

36. http://www.brazzil.com/p122mar03.htm (accessed: August 9, 2009) and http://www.streetswing.com/histmain/z3bossa.htm (accessed: August 11, 2009).

37. John Charles Chasteen, *National Rhythms, African Roots: The Deep History of Latin American Popular Dance* (Albuquerque, NM: University of New Mexico Press, 2004), 6.

38. Steward, 8.

39. Ed Morales, *The Latin Beat: The Rhythms and Roots of Latin Music from Bossa Nova to Salsa and Beyond* (Cambridge, MA: Da Capro Press, 2003), Introduction, xiii.

40. Steward, 13.

41. Steward, 97–98.

42. Steward, 11.

43. Steward, 61.

44. Steward, 14.

45. Steward, 73.

46. Amy Morris, from: "Zumba: Newest exercise craze mixes Latin music, dance moves for aerobic workout" (TCPALM) Monday, April 7, 2008, http://news.zumba.com/news/ (accessed: January 12, 2010).

47. Judy Fortin, CNN Medical Correspondent. cnn.com/2008/HEALTH/diet.fitness/09/22/hm.zumba.dance.exercise/index (accessed: June 2, 2009).

5

Latin Exhibition and Art Dance

South America [is] a part of the world so rich in dance and so bursting with dancers that it is hard to understand why it has not yet become the world's centre.

Dame Margot Fonteyn[1]

Halfway between art and entertainment, in the middle ground between the formality of competition ballroom and the informality of social dancing, is the freestyle world of exhibition Latin dance. Meant to be watched as much as to be danced by amateurs and professionals (sometimes together in pro-am events), this venue has clearly influenced the way social Latin dances change with new and exciting steps and figures, costumes, and rhythmic responses to the music. And it doesn't just stay on a conventional dance floor, either; some of the most exciting Latin exhibition dancing on view is ice dancing.

Latin dances bring a wealth of dynamic variation, precision, stylish flair, and expressive range to competition ballroom dancing, since 1988 called DanceSport. Both Spanish Latin and tropical Latin dances make excellent exhibition material, and high-speed competitive tropical Latin dances require exact choreographic precision in footwork, holds, figures, and Latin motion, in addition to expressive musicality. While those who dance for pleasure enjoy a range of styles defined by tempo and rhythmic patterns, dance competition requires classification of dance styles with specific and uniform criteria for judging valuations. But although ballroom competition dancing is strictly performed by couples, exhibition dances may also be performed in single- or mixed-gender groups, as well as wheelchairs.[2]

International Standard and Latin dances, and the American Smooth and Rhythm dances, constitute the two different categories of ballroom competition that comprises Latin dances. International Standard and Latin dances are characterized by a high degree of formality and precision of execution. Judging is based on specific standards that were set in 1924 by the Imperial Society of Teachers of Dancing. The International Standard includes the waltz, Viennese waltz, fox-trot, quick-step, and the tango, while International Standard Latin Dances include the cha-cha, jive, paso doble, samba, and rumba. American Smooth and Rhythm dances encourage a little more individual interpretation and athleticism, especially in front of television audiences. They are less restrictive and more amenable to commercial dance studio instruction for the general public, through such venues as the Arthur Murray and Fred Astaire franchises.

In competition, American Smooth dances include the same dances as the International Standard except for the quick-step, which was dropped because it was considered too complex. But that doesn't mean American Smooth dances are tame by comparison, as they allow partners to break away from the traditional closed position into a variety of solo, synchronized (hands joined or not), and side-by-side variations. American Rhythm dances include the cha-cha, swing (instead of jive), rumba, and samba, with occasional additions of mambo, bolero, or merengue. The difference between the International Standard and the American Smooth is further marked in the cut of the woman's costume; while the International Standard requires formal ball gowns, the quick turns and more flashy moves in American Smooth call for slit gowns and dramatic bodices.

Spain is the European origin of these dances, and ever since the country defined itself by culture and language, it has been viewed as richly endowed with many sacred (strictly controlled by the Roman Catholic Church into "processionals") and secular social dance styles. No one is exactly sure when or where couples' dancing (with a man and a woman holding hands) first appeared, but it was speculated that it probably was a court dance innovation out of Provence, France, as part of the courtly love and troubadour traditions.[3] But courtly love and troubadours were ideas out of Spanish Moorish poems and songs, as the North African Islamic Empire spread across the narrow Strait of Gibraltar and into Europe from AD 711 until they were finally driven out of Spain by the Catholic Queen Isabella and King Ferdinand (the same year, Christopher Columbus was sent on his famous voyage to find a passage west to the riches of the Far East).

The musical connection with Spanish Latin dance lies in the basic habanera style, but elements of the habanera are also found in the United States; among them "rockabilly" music.[4] The style also became popular in Mexico and the United States following Sebastian Yradier's 1884 song, *La Paloma*. And groups of musicians called orquestas típicas ("typical orchestras") first accompanied Cuban contradanzas with a habanera pattern. Then by incorporating a cinquillo (or, a very fast repeating five-beat pattern in a single bar as played in percussion or stride piano) these European-style dances were "tropicalized" into danzón improvisations.[5] The habanera was so well-known throughout Europe that it was picked up by the French classical composer Georges Bizet (1838–1875) for his "Spanish" (sung in French: 1875) opera, *Carmen*.

Recorded art dancing in the Spanish Latin mode has been around since the publication of one of Europe's first dancing manuals by Juan de Esquivel Navarro (who was the dancing master to Philip IV) in 1642. And exhibition Latin dancing seems to have gotten off to a good start in 1845, when the dance team of Felix García and Manuela Perea presented the *Bolero de la Caleta* in London. Soloists also toured Spanish dances; Pepita de Oliva's long, unbound tresses created a sensation as she danced a variety of "Spanish" dances and played the castanets across Europe in 1853.

But it was the *Cachucha*, performed by the Austrian-born dance artist Fanny Elssler (1810–1884) in *Le Diable Boiteux*, that drove audiences in the United States wild. Elssler's tour of America was to have lasted three months, but she ended up staying for three years. Everywhere she went, enthusiastic crowds spread carpets of flowers before her. Sessions of Congress closed for every one of her 1840 Washington, DC performances. But even before Elssler, audiences in the United States seem to have gotten at least a glimmer of a tango. Philadelphia dance theatre performer Charles Durang (1794–1870) described a tango danced to waltz time music that he had learned from teachers in Paris and London.[6]

As aristocratic relatives, it is understandable that Spanish Latin and the ballet are so compatible. The form and movements of flamenco

Members of the Venezuelan dance company "Mariara" perform a Samba dance on the grounds of the world exposition Expo 2000 in Hanover, Germany, Thursday, June 22, 2000. (AP Photo/Jan Bauer.)

codified by the escuela bolero (bolero school) set the standard of Spanish dances and the level of skill the dancers should maintain. The escuela also incorporated exercises and sequences from the ballet.[7] Popular "character" dance numbers were often inserted into full-length ballets, such as the bolero-like "Chocolate" in the 1892 *The Nutcracker* (Ivanov-Petipa), the all-time favorite Christmas ballet in the United States. The 1869 Petipa ballet *Don Quixote* (1869) includes a variety of Spanish folk and classical dances. Modern ballet takes a turn in the Spanish mode with Roland Petit's *Carmen* (1949), a takeoff on Bizet's opera. Pretty much any ballet training anywhere in the world today must include Russian, Polish, and Spanish character dances adapted for the stage from folk dances. While these standards were set in Europe, the United States adopted them wholesale (and imported European ballet dancers and dancing masters) until modern dance began to be taken seriously as art, sometime around 1910.

Meanwhile, even outside vaudeville, Latin dance pairs were going strong in all kinds of places. The team of Veloz and Yolanda continued to performed Latin dances in the 1930s as part of Latin music reviews in hotels, cabarets, and ballrooms. The Mambo Aces Andy Vásquez and Joe Centeno featured virtuoso routines together, mixing Latin with lindy and Charleston steps, very much as the top-billed vaudevillians the Nickolas Brothers did. Millie Distafano and "Cuban Pete" Aguilar splashed rumbas, tap, and modern dance figures into their exhibition routines, which mambo contestants at the Palladium were quick to make their own.

Latin Dance on the Vaudeville Boards

The highbrow elite of the ballet world wasn't the only home that Latin dances found in the United States. Americans have always been very good at entertaining themselves, and the vaudeville stage (which ran approximately from 1880 to 1932, when the last vaudeville theatre closed) was the perfect venue for it. It was in vaudeville that the United States settled into defining its immigrant, urban, and industrialized image to itself after the Civil War, right up until World War I. And that included the most outrageous stereotype comedies of the new arrivals, mainly Germans, Jews, Italians, and the Irish. Blackface acts from minstrel shows (white performers who blackened their faces with a combination of lard mixed with burned cork) took care of African-American Jim Crow spoofs; Afro-Cuban routines were "jungle dances," and "Mexicans" occasionally wandered in and out of scenes wearing oversized sombreros and strumming a guitar. No ethnic group was spared; a white ukulele player even painted his skin yellow and wore a "Chinese" costume for his act.

The battleground between high art and low art was never more clearly defined than on the vaudeville touring circuits, which ranged widely in the quality of the theatre, bar, or dance hall. The Orpheum, Pantages, Loew, and Keith circuits featured high-class acts, usually imported from Europe. Along with successful variety acts, these circuits might bring monologues from Shakespeare's plays, opera songs, or short ballet programs of the Ballets Russes (a group of Russian ballet artists displaced by the revolution, who were usually camped out in Paris, but which brought the fabulous ballerina Anna Pavlova to the United States). Top-billed vaudeville dance acts could earn up to $250 a week.[8] But there was also the horrific T. O. B. A. circuit, which booked black jazz and blues musicians as well as other acts for black audiences into the south.

Several Latin musicians toured in vaudeville; unfortunately, their names are lost. Unless they could pass for white, they were probably sent round on the T. O. B. A. circuit along with other black (or "colored") performers who often performed the ever-popular cake walk.[9]

More typically, however, white vaudevillians performed as exotic dancers—Egyptians, Arabs, Chinese, Spaniards, etc.; it didn't really matter. The first week that the Prescott, Arizona, Elks Opera House opened to vaudeville in 1910, a Spanish dancer named Mary Reed was listed among the acts.[10] The Paris gutter dance called the apache (which, especially as it was performed in the United States included steps and figures from the equally disreputable maxixie and tango) created a sensation among tourists visiting cabarets and dance halls, and it wasn't long before it hit vaudeville. As presented by one Giovanni Molasso (something of an Italian comedian), the apache made a startling exhibition style dance, though it was often under attack by moralists as "bestial." Still, dancers pulling each other's hair or violently throwing each other across the stage was well within the spirit of vaudeville dancing, which had to produce something physically acrobatic in order to catch the eye of audiences. In any case, the apache was popular enough that a couple of American dancers saw some gain in copying it so they could turn it into a stunt dance called *Vampire Dance* (1909).[11]

Someone with the stage name of "Carmencita" did a cachucha and a fandango with castanets at Koster & Bial's in New York City to some acclaim in 1890, and between movie engagements, Mae Murray and Clifton Webb appeared in the vaudeville review *Society Dances* with maxixies and tangos.[12] But Latin dancers on vaudeville weren't all novelty acts with an exotic note of the burlesque; some pretty serious dancers also worked the boards from time to time. The exhibition duo of Maurice Mouvet and Florence Walton performed vaudeville maxixies and tangos prior to World War I, an activity that didn't seem to hurt Mouvet's reputation as a top-notch dance instructor at all.

Later, the more well-known pair of Vernon and Irene Castle also went on circuit, but Irene Castle's memoirs made it clear that they'd only do that when there was no other way to meet the bills. As always, there were many imitations of the most successful acts, including the Orpheum circuit pair of Ivy and Douglas Crane, who were billed as "The Vernon and Irene Castle of the West." Even Fred Astaire got his start at a very young age dancing on the vaudeville circuit with his sister Adele, despite being labeled a "lounge lizard," or "gigolo," as male exhibition dancers were commonly called at the time. Many Broadway and Hollywood performers got their first big breaks in vaudeville.

The track was not only effective for entertainment artists; serious artists also found their way through vaudeville, although reluctantly. American modern dance pioneers Ruth St. Denis (1880–1968) and Ted Shawn (1891–1972) toured vaudeville to make ends meet even as they struggled in their early years to get the public to accept them as serious dance artists. Shawn was no stranger to the popular dances of his day; he and an earlier partner opened the first tango teas in Los Angeles at the Angelus Hotel in 1912.[13] St. Denis started her public dancing as an attractive, limber skirt dancer in dime museum shows and vaudeville. Together, St. Denis and Shawn created the first American art dance company and school of Denishawn, and kicked it off with a 1914 vaudeville performance in Paducah, Kentucky, in a program that included a maxixie and a tango.

Still, Denishawn would get out of vaudeville as quickly as possible, leaving the entertainment of novelty dances to the masses. After all, the goal was to create an original form of American art dance that was as high-class as the ballet. Latin couples dancing was not only familiar to audiences that had danced them socially, but provided a high-tone link between the popular and the artistic. In time, other Spanish-style dances choreographed by Shawn were added to the Denishawn concert repertoire, one of which introduced the very young Martha Graham as Shawn's partner in his 1921 *Malagueña*. At the same time, tango lessons were offered in the Denishawn dance studio franchise. But only Spanish Latin dances were acceptable to teach or perform; any with the slightest hint of African origins, or even a suggestion of a pelvic move, were not. St. Denis particularly had struggled far too hard and too long to make her audiences take her seriously as a dance artist to risk slipping back into low and common entertainment classification. With Spanish Latin dances firmly entrenched in both the professional dance company and supporting school of Denishawn, it could be said that with their first steps together on an American concert stage, Latin dance and American modern dance made a compatible partnership.[14]

Skirt Dancing with Latin

While tropical Latin dances were not as evident in vaudeville as
Spanish Latin dances were, skirt dancing was a pretty popular
vaudeville routine. The basic idea was that the skirt dancer held her
skirts out and moved them around as she danced, affording a glance
of her twinkling ankles and maybe a knee or two, something rather
naughtily risqué in Victorian eyes. And it also didn't hurt if the basic
vaudeville skirt dancer was limber enough to perform backbends,
flips, and the splits, just as they reputedly did in the outrageous
cancan dances way off in Paris, France.

Skirt dancing first showed up in the British music halls around 1876. It
wasn't a difficult dance to do, although ballet dancer Kate Vaughn made
it into a charming dance at the Gaiety Theatre of London. While skirt
dancing entertainment had been around as long as men have been willing
to pay money to watch women throw up their skirts, Vaughn elevated the
basic attraction by choreographing her skirts into a variety of shapes and
patterns—"basket weave," "serpentine," "butterfly" or "flower
blossom," just to name a few. Her dance was quickly appropriated by
Americans Amelia Glover and Bessie McCoy for vaudeville novelty dancing, which hit its peak of popularity in the United States between 1888
and 1910. For a while, skirt dancing was a social ballroom dance in its
own right. Girls' finishing schools included instruction in "graceful and
tasteful" skirt dancing as part of what went into the creation of a refined
lady.[15] Even Irene Castle studied skirt dancing as part of her training.

Several Latin folk and classical dances from Spain across
the Western Hemisphere also caught that eye with fanciful skirt
manipulations, and for this reason they are often easily adapted from
folk to concert stage dances. The one that comes quickest to mind is
the *Mexican Hat Dance*, a jarabe-style folk dance that has been a
perennial tourist pleaser during which the ladies elegantly swish their
skirts, and in one figure, the gentleman takes the hem of her skirt and
holds it out to each side as they shine forward and back again. The
haughty flamenco dancer also lifts and moves her ruffled train from
side to side during her zapateos (fancy footwork) section. And an
elegantly-gowned cumbia lady holds her skirt across herself from side
to side as she weaves back and forth around her partner. For Puerto
Rican bomba y plena, plantation-style dances, the ample skirts of the
lady are ruffled like birds' feathers as she dances forward to—or back

from—her partner. The skirt bells out around her as she twirls, and froths around her knees as she kneels on the ground.

Whether or not skirt dancing and Latin dances that use the skirt as a dance prop are linked, it is certain that the attraction of both lies in the eye of the beholder, often male. And oddly enough, skirt dancing provided an important stepping stone toward the creation of a new, modern American concert dance to rival the European-based ballet. Three American women are credited with that honor; two of whom got their start in vaudeville as skirt dancers. While Isadora Duncan went in for the exotica of classical Greek statuary for her onstage look, Ruth St. Denis and Loie Fuller (1862–1928) experimented with the visual effect of the female form made abstract in fabric. St. Denis moved on into the exotic appeal of Far East orientalism, in which the full skirts of a Hindu goddess rippled around her rapidly-spinning body (as in her 1906 *Radha*). But Fuller explored the potential of silk cloth manipulated more like a stage prop than a costume. She was the first dancer/choreographer to darken her theatre and splash the new electric lights in changing colors across seemingly endless yards of fabric.[16] It is ironic that skirt dancing, originally performed for the male gaze, should be the means by which these dancer/choreographers would wrest control of artistic production out of patriarchal hands and into their own, resulting in American modern concert dance.

Latin Exhibition Dance Duos and Dance Studio Frachising

St. Denis and Shawn made an attractive dance pair—not only in art dances, but also concert versions of Spanish dances. At the same time, the Denishawn dance instruction franchise (one in Los Angeles and one in New York City) went two ways. On one level, anyone willing to pay the price could be taught tango basics by the handsome Shawn in a private or small-group lesson. Or, professional Broadway and Hollywood actors and dancers could obtain expert coaching at Denishawn in everything from Latin dancing to how to convincingly fall down stairs. And in yet another context, the franchise advertized that St. Denis herself (for a fee, of course) would teach a performer the steps and movements of one of her own solos, advise on the creation of an appropriate costume, and then grant permission for that student—once she had achieved an acceptable competence in performing it—the certified right to that dance and its music to perform it on stage. It was very clever; a kind of multiple copying of St. Denis' elegant persona live on stage through a corps of individual dancers performing in her very image.[17]

While Denishawn struggled for full concert art status as well as economic survival, exhibition Spanish and tropical Latin dance pairs performed in cabarets, floor shows, and restaurants as well as in vaudeville, on Broadway, and in the movies. Unlike upper-class assembly balls of the 1800s into the 1900s, attended only by invitation, these urban venues offered a night's entertainment and participation in the latest dance steps to anyone who could pay the price. This shift turned social dance—and the Latin varieties along with it—from a class distinction into a mercantile one. And exhibition pairs that had become famous in performance were quick to capitalize on that option.

"By 1912, numerous New York restaurants remodeled their dining floors to place diner's tables in close proximity to bands and exhibition dancers who performed at the center of the floor."[18] Those who had the means to tour had an even greater audience base, and diners could observe the dress, the steps, and the form of exhibition dancers at close range, and then take to the floor themselves in imitation. Capitalizing on that urge, dance pairs also franchised the business of dance studio instruction based on their popularity in performing.

The most well-known of these in the United States were Vernon and Irene Castle, who spread the tango and maxixie as respectable (that is, without the Latin motion of tropical Latin dances) ballroom forms through their countrywide tours and teaching everywhere they went. Although the assembly balls were vanishing, the Castles were highly sensitive to criticism that called popular dances "immoral." Upon the request of New England socialite Mrs. S. Fish, the Castles choreographed and danced an "innovation" tango, which, like the "innovation" waltz, required that partners have no physical contact between them.

This is a challenging condition, especially for a tango, because it is one of the few social dances in which the man and the woman perform different steps. But propriety above all was the Castle motto, and passion of any kind had no place in social dancing. As Irene Castle said, "If Vernon had once looked at me with anything suggestive in his expression, I think we both would have burst out laughing."[19] Later in movie dancing, this "hands off" partnering became a staple of numbers performed by Fred Astaire and Ginger Rogers, from tap to salsa to their particular version of the carioca.

Movies like *Roberta*, starring Rogers and Astaire in Latin dances, encouraged audiences to sign up at dance studios. (AP Photo.)

In true entrepreneurial form, the Castles not only performed and demonstrated these dances at the best hotels and cabarets in the United States and Europe, but established their own cabaret; they also fed the dance craze with articles on proper dance in magazines, and established their own New York City dance school, Castle House, in 1913. They published their own dance manual, *Modern Dancing*, in 1914, in which they stressed the grace and beauty of refined couple dances.

But not all social dance studios were based on famous pairs; in fact, the two most well-known names belong to men: Arthur Murray and Fred Astaire. The very clever and competent Arthur Murray (1895–1991) was born in East Harlem with the name Moses Teichman. Murray got his start teaching dance at Castle Hall. Being the acute businessman that he was, Murray established his own dance studio in Atlanta, Georgia, and then in 1924 moved back to New York City. There he not only provided one-on-one instruction in all the social dances of the day, but set up what urned out to be an extremely profitable mail order business selling his own devised diagrams on how to dance the steps. More than 300 Arthur Murray studios were going all across the United States by 1960.[20] The Chicago Arthur Murray studios proudly announced complete facilities for learning merengue, salsa, or tango to the heart's content. Glowing testimonials in Arthur Murray dance studio advertisements proclaimed the miraculous transformation of the socially challenged into swans of sophistication with, "How I Became Popular Overnight!"[21]

The Fred Astaire Studios also offered salsa along with all the other popular social Latin dances for special events like weddings, competition ballroom events, and the social enjoyment of groups hosting each other at "open floor night" events, where partners destined to find one another over a rumba or samba could meet. Coaches today even offer choreography and coaching for couples appearing on the TV show, *So You Think You Can Dance.*

Fred Astaire was legendary for demanding exact precision in every one of his dance routines. Upon his retirement in 1947, he put the same attention to detail into his Fred Astaire Dance Studios at Park Avenue in New York City. Although he sold the franchise in 1966, his name still not only attracts the thousands of moviegoers who would like to learn how to "dance like Fred," but also some top-notch coaching talent to the studios. Not to be outdone by its closest rival, Arthur Murray Studios, the Fred Astaire chain also carries a full line of dance wear, including eleven different styles of FADS (Fred Astaire Dance Studio) men's shoes, instructional tapes, music, and more to meet every need of the aspiring dancer. As its website proclaims, "Dancing enhances every aspect of your life. You'll look good to others as they watch you dance, take pride in knowing that your partner enjoys dancing with you, and—most importantly—feel great about yourself as you dance."[22]

Latin Dance in the Movies

The expressive potential and ranges of emotional complexities inherent in all Latin dances were not lost on photographers even as early as the mid-1800s, and silent experimental films—which were intent on capturing the reality and the fantasy of every aspect of human 'life—were equally quick to capture Latin dance on film. One of the most prevailing means by which Latin social dances spread across the United States was through the movies.

While the tango took a sensual, steamy turn around the cinematic dance floor with Latin heartthrob Rudolph Valentino romancing some mesmerized beauty in early silent films, Hollywood moviegoers of the 1930s were also briefly treated to the elegant beauty of Mexican native Dolores Del Rio, who spanned from silent into talking films playing sultry international women from Rio de Janeiro to Havana. Her willowy, statuesque figure, draped in clinging gowns, suggested the ultimate in worldly sophistication and the exotic mystery of an eternally elusive paradise.[23] The attractive appearances of Del Rio in urban paradises "south of the border" in such films as *Flying Down to Rio* (1933), and *In Caliente* (1935) may have encouraged North Americans wealthy enough to do so to plan their vacations in relatively inexpensive luxury. Part of their leisure was spent in the dance clubs of these cities, where they learned to rumba, samba, or tango the night away.

The demand for the catchy, smooth syncopations of the music to go with these dances also began to bring north the musicians who could play them, both live and broadcast over the radio. Dance studios eager to keep pace with the latest trends also rushed to be the first to offer "authentic" lessons in these newest dances. Latin music in the media got a significant boost in the late 1920s, when Cuban band leader Xavier Cugat and his orchestra brought Latin music to the Coconut Grove of Los Angeles. Quick to pick up on the exotic appeal of Latin dance and music, nearby Hollywood made the most of likeable—and marketable to white movie-goers—musicians such as Cugat and his vocalist, Desi Arnaz.

Arnaz also brought a touch of Latin music now and then into American living rooms with one of the most popular (1951 to 1957 on CBS) TV shows of all time, *I Love Lucy*. This kind of exposure to the Latin beat put the "bug in the ear/the tingle in the feet" for others outside urban Latino enclaves. But the fame and fortune that Hollywood brought Latin musicians and dancers came with a price. "In the early forties many Latin musicians objected to the bastardization of their music. Xavier Cugat wrote in *Esquire* in 1942 that the phoney rhumba was encouraged by President Roosevelt. He described it as 'a good neighbor scheme to make Yankees love Latins and vice versa.' "[24]

However, the tropical Latin social dances had their greatest surge of popularity on North American dance floors as a result of film media response to the Good Neighbor Policy of the 1940s. A propaganda campaign through the media (primarily film, but also in advertizing imagery and radio) by the U.S. government, the Good Neighbor Policy was intended to prevent Latin American countries from selling their considerable resources to Germany, Italy, or Japan during World War II.

Happy to comply with government support in not only promoting the purchases of war bonds by the American public, but by also projecting a cheerful, light, and firm friendship between North and South America, movie studios put out an astounding number of Latin films chock full of sambas, rumbas, cariocas, and other flashy dance numbers. As sales and promotion of Hollywood films in Europe were dwindling at the time, Hollywood jumped at the chance to offer a new and different style of musical comedy that appealed not only to novelty-hungry audiences at home, but also to new audiences in the urban centers of South America. Elaborately-staged musicals in which characters from both cultures joined together in song and dance symbolized a unity of sociopolitical direction and purpose, all wrapped up together in a lighthearted festival holiday setting.[25]

Taking a cue from the immediate successes of 20th Century Fox's Latin musical comedy hits of 1940 (*Down Argentine Way*) and 1941 (*Weekend in Havana* and *That Night in Rio*), other studios rushed to cash in on the Latin dance boom. The most famous and highly-paid actress of the time was "the Brazilian Bombshell" Carmen Miranda, who sang and danced in elaborate and suggestive costumes (even though her bellybutton was covered with a flesh-colored bandage) and "Spanglished" her way through a witty and fast-paced dialogue as a comic character.

Although Brazilian, Miranda portrayed stereotypically hot-tempered, exotic women from any Latin American country as required in the musical story while she enthusiastically participated in Hollywood's Good Neighbor films of the 1940s and early '50s. Miranda was never allowed out of her narrow typecast for more serious roles. Still, she performed some of the most well-known samba numbers in film history, making full use of samba's side-to-side locomotive jauntiness for the essentially two-dimensional camera's-eye view. Each time Miranda sambaed her way across the screen, she seemed to welcome the audience to get up and join the dance. And dance they did, filling the

Top Hollywood Latin singer/dancer Carmen Miranda in the 1940s. (AP Photo.)

floors of studios, dance clubs, and social events halls with long conga lines and the sounds of maracas and bongo drums, and throwing out plenty of Latin motion in the process.

Even today, samba is "the good-time beat that just doesn't die," especially in the media. For example, the samba music for the climax of the Elvis Presley 1964 MGM movie *Viva Las Vegas* featured a rousing samba that has recently found an equally "rousing" reincarnation as the music in a television commercial for a "male enhancement product."[26]

Spanish and tropical Latin dances informed, and were informed by, the two-dimensional eye of the camera that implied a three-dimensional reality. The iconic moment (or pause) occurs as if posing for a photograph is an indispensable feature of modern culture—from advertizing to high schoolers posing in the hallways for the benefit of the opposite sex—and everything in between that connects the two. Because Latin dances especially allow for "iconic" pauses (that is, moments in which the dancers stop moving, in a dramatically-composed image designed for the audience's point of view), Latin dancers participate in this pattern of "fame and gain" with instant recognition through public exhibition.

The tango is probably the best example, for it is a dance to do, and a dance to be seen doing; that is, it displays the dancers to an audience. Smooth, sharp, and streamlined efficiency of movement (often called "gracefulness"), essential to the tango look, fits well with the popular Art Deco (1930s through 1940s in the United States),—with smoothed-back hair for both men and women, clothes that cling to the body and do not in any way interfere with the quick changes of direction, and a sense of powerful, dynamic, and speedy access from one area of space to another. It is no coincidence that Art Deco and tango dances became immensely popular at the same time, as they compliment the aesthetics of strength, speed, athleticism, and progressivism.

The particularly tango-like dynamic of sudden stillness to vigorous movement and back again has been exploited in modern concert art dance and on film throughout the twentieth century. Vogueing is a skill achieved through abrupt isolations, or opposing movements by direction, rhythm, or speed performed simultaneously in different parts of a dancer's body. The technique is perfected by anyone seriously engaged in Latin dance, as well as jazz dance, modern art dance, and the ballet. Striking that captive, iconic pose (as if posing for a still camera shot in a magazine like *Vogue*) continues to transfix audiences of all genres of movies, particularly the fantasy action/inaction of such films as *The Matrix* (1999).

Capoeira and Breaking

The young man quite literally appears to leap up and hurl himself toward the sidewalk, falling and rolling on his side. Then swinging his arms and legs into a spiral, he vaults himself onto the top of his head, and spins a few revolutions upside down. With a kick, and a push with one hand against the hard surface, he rights himself on his feet again. A ring of observer/participants encircle him, urging, clapping, and shouting.

Someone watching breaking (or, break dancing) for the first time would be simply amazed that anyone could do such a thing without injury. While it is true injuries have happened, and even one death when a breaker broke his neck in 1982, proper practice and protection of knees and elbows renders injury less likely. A sturdy pair of sneakers is also required, since breaking takes place on a hard—never a soft—surface; breakers toprock (steps opening the breaker's style), downrock (footwork), perform power moves, freezes (gravity-defying poses), and suicides (falling). On their feet or on their heads, braced off in three-point balances or in kick-leaps, breakers use their centers of balance, a three-point contact with hands and feet, and the constancy of gravity to express self-empowerment.

On a par with stunt skateboarding and the more recent fad of "parkour" (that is, the method of "finding new ways of moving through your environment" such as walking up railings or swinging on tree branches) the high athleticism of breaking is almost more stunt than dance. While street-side breaking is measured out to hip-hop/funk from a boom box—and other music such as soul or jazz also suits—it is still a deep, inner-city, and largely male-dominated sport dance (although there are b-girls, too). The names of some of the figures are pretty colorful; air flares, head spins, the dizzy run, top rock, apple jack, and windmill, among others.

Breaking is exhibition dancing at the extreme—at the edge of where dance ends and violence begins; when rival street gangs competed to win in dancing, it was not unusual for a real fight to start. And the muscle memory required to do this kind of dancing is the same as that required to move through a hand-to-knife gang fight. While breaking itself has waned from the mainstream eye in recent years, it is still a strong influence on the high-powered dance moves in rap videos and action movies.

Credited with having sprung up in the Bronx during the disco era of the 1970s, breaking gets its name from the breaks in disco music sets as the records were changed, and, "dancers would feel the air with movements corresponding to the break."[27] Disco dances may have contributed to the development of breaking, along with some Far East martial arts moves made popular in action movies. Each performer practices his own moves, figures out how best to transition from one figure to the next, and learns new ones from others. But the performance of the sequence itself is improvised. Although it is suggested that breaking got its start from the athletics of the lindy hop or Charleston, its philosophy of movement to music links it to the Brazilian fight dance of capoeira.

Capoeira is the unarmed warrior's art, a strengthening of mind and body for any challenge that is to come, merging Brazilian frevo music (European polkas or marches, played like a swing jazz band) with Angolan martial arts. Though traditionally a man's preserve, women and children have also entered the roda (the circular performing space defined by a ring of observers who may also participate in turn).

As an activity filled with heroic defiance against slavery, capoeira is a ritualized fight dance strongly influenced by African male virtuoso dancing in which performers/combatants take turns. When the Dutch invaded Brazil in 1624–1630, slaves escaped from farms and sugar mills into forests to organize themselves into quilomos, where they developed the art of capoeira to defend themselves with their bare hands and feet against recapture. The word "capoeira" comes from the name of the brushwood in which they hid. Outlawed in 1890, capoeira was reinstated due to the efforts of Mestre Bimba, who persuaded Brazilian authorities that the dance was an integral part of Brazilian culture.[28]

Jorge Guerra, left, and Joshua Granger play each other in a game of capoeira as the rest of the Gingarte Capoeira Group of Chicago looks on, Monday, November 11, 2002, in Chicago. Capoeira is a Brazilian martial art that combines music, dance, acrobatics, and fighting. (AP Photo/Brandi Jade Thomas.)

The songs which accompany the dance are of a great variety: instruction, historical information, encouragement, ethical advice, legends, or comical motifs. Early in the 1900s there were very few women in capoiera. But since the 1970s, along with a change in the song lyrics from an attitude of suspiciousness against women to one including them as part of the struggle for freedom and respect, more women have joined the roda. Today, women make up 40 percent of students and participants in well over 2,000 schools worldwide, and there are now four San Francisco capoeira masters who are women.[29]

Athletic and fast, capoeira depends upon the inventiveness and physical capabilities of individual dancers and the interdependence of a pair of partners/combatants who refer to each other as camara or comrade.[30] Traditional figures in capoeira include the negation, the stingray's tail (rabo de arraia), the whip (chiblata), the half-moon (meia luna), the sissors (tesoura), cartweel (au), sweep (rasteira), and head butt (cabeçada). Other moves for this dance-fight are both basic and stunning; ginga is a kind of "readiness movement" in which the dancers sway from side to side and move in balance-steady directions with deeply bent knees, ever-ready to dart in any conceivable direction to throw or evade a thrust.[31]

Overall, it is something like a human version of cockfighting, all painstakingly practiced under the watchful eye of a master who urges the philosophy of respect, safety, freedom, and malicia (the art of tricking your opponent into an indefensible position). Capoeira dancing transposed into large metro venues of the United States contributed prominently to the popularity of breaking and other virtuoso street dance forms.

Wheelchair Latin Dancing

How do you dance in a wheelchair? For that matter, how do you play basketball from a chair? Persistence, the heart of a warrior, and a sturdy will to achieve the nearly impossible, makes it possible. Of course, there are limits that must be recognized—some firm and some that can be revised—the trick is to know the differences. Standard competition Latin dancing is not possible to a wheelchair couple because the strict adherence to form and steps can only be performed by ambulatory couples. However, the freer form allowed in exhibition permits a wide range of individual expression, and there are wheelchair DanceSport competitions with their own sets of rules.

The Bella Studio of Performing Arts in Kansas City now includes Groovability (groovability.com), a wheelchair ballroom dance group started by Chris Pruitt (who is ambulatory) and Joanne Fluke (chaired), who are also dance partners. Their newly-formed group currently has eight wheelchair students, in their teens to mid-thirties. Several of them performed on August 15, 2009, in the Exhibition Solo Division of the Heart of America Ballroom Dance Championships in Kansas City.

Pruitt and Fluke began their collaboration with a samba, which they practiced together for about two weeks before presenting it in public. Since then, the two of them have included other ambulatory and wheelchair members, and their exhibition dances have been dynamic, expressive, and engaging experiences for both dancers and audiences.

In an interview on August 14, 2009, Pruitt and Fluke were asked about challenges facing the disabled that most ambulatory people take for granted and seldom think about. Getting out and into social situations in nonthreatening and leveling ways to find techniques for becoming invested in life, rather than passively watching it flow past (one of the main barriers), was the first point they made. According to Fluke, "The issue with dancing is that it breaks down those barriers between the disability community and the non-disability community —that's one of my big passions. Groovability tries to get out at least once a month to other dance clubs and studios that have open dance floor night and interact."

But why Latin dancing, and how is it they chose the samba over other styles of ballroom dance to start? The answer from Pruitt was that Latin allows for "a little in-your-face craziness" that the smooth styles don't permit; it "releases the self" into the movement of the partnership, as one leads and the other follows—and then the roles reverse. As Fluke stated, "The other ballroom styles are too prim and proper. In the samba, I could flirt; it's feisty and fun, sassy, and playful."

Adding to that sense of freedom, Pruitt added that Latin provides a dramatic tension between restraint and control, sort of like a Dr. Jekyll and Mr. Hyde pair of opposites. As he put it, "The actual connections [in Latin dancing] are electrical. The differences between [a samba and a cha-cha] are expressed in the rhythm-to-body movement," something the wheelchair itself allows with directions forward and back, sideways, turns and twists, or even a little 'bounce,' a kind of twitching or jerking of the wheels. And, as Pruitt proudly stated,

"Joanne can do her [torso] isolations in the chair. I am not moving *her*; *we* are moving [together]."

A significant issue addressed in Latin dancing between ambulatory and chaired dancers is control; a matter of who is leading and who is following. Fluke said the hardest part for her was to allow someone else to be in control. "A lot of us in the disability community, when we think of independence, we think it means doing it yourself, but allowing other people to help you so you can be independent [is the goal], whereby you can also help the other person, too." Pruitt takes it from a leadership point of view; "Independence means being the best that you can be individually to play your part. A true leader is not someone who makes things happen. A true leader will allow, or will make room, or will encourage, or direct or motivate the other person to do well." So the swing of momentum between partners is not only physical, but emotional and psychological as well as that control; that leading/following, push/pull, attraction/rejection of Latin dance flows between them.

Added to that, both Fluke and Pruitt say that eye contact also keeps the partners engaged and connected psychically. And that eye contact between a seated and standing partner is at a diagonal to the audience's visual "picture" of the dance, rather than parallel to the dance floor as would be more or less the case with two standing partners. Especially in the Latin dances, this angle is advantageously explored to emphasize the dramatic sexual complexities of a Latin dance.

Chris Pruitt and JoAnne Fluke of Groovability, Kansas City, Mo., strike a dramatic exhibition Samba pose. (© Chris Pruitt. Reprinted with permission.)

Pruitt further explained that the lead/follow partnering in Latin dance is not fully understood unless the roles are occasionally changed; that is, unless the woman (in this case the chair partner) leads and the man (the ambulatory partner) follows. He said he could not ask his chaired partner to do something he himself had not done. To that effect, Pruitt put himself into a wheelchair for three days, not using his legs in any way just to experience for himself over a brief period of time what his partner had to deal with on a permanent basis.

There are many physical things to learn in the process of learning a wheelchair Latin dance; there are failures, falls, trips, tumbles, and injuries. The ambulatory partner must be able to step around the wheels so that the sculptural presentation of two bodies (not to mention the movements of the wheelchair itself) is not impeded. Close holds are not possible, unless the chaired partner is lifted up and out of the chair to be carried. The chair itself may be moved by the ambulatory partner or by the chair partner, and part of the skill and art of this dancing lies in the smooth transitions of this force of momentum passing between them.

While lateral (side-to-side) movements such as a grapevine pattern are not possible in a wheelchair, a surprising range of up, down, forward, and back movements are available, especially as the wheelchair itself provides a "launch pad" trajectory from which the dancer escapes, even briefly, and then returns. The wheelchair may be tilted back into a dip; the ambulatory partner may shift from standing to kneeling or even lying on the floor to assume support over the ground. The smooth transitions between "in wheelchair" gesture and locomotion and "out of wheelchair" dancing helps the flow of the dance. And best of all while dancing, the chair is always there, and yet not there—an aid instead of an impediment, a flow of locomotion instead of a limitation, not just for the dancers themselves, but also for those watching the dance.

Notes

1. Dame Margot Fonteyn, *The Magic of Dance* (Knopf, 1979), 315.
2. Author's unpublished observation notes from August 14–16, 2009, Kansas City Heart of America Ballroom Dance Championships in Kansas City.
3. Gerald Jonas, *Dancing: the Pleasure, Power, and Art of Movement* (New York: Harry N. Abrams, Inc., 1998), 50.
4. Ed Morales, *The Latin Beat: The Rhythms and Roots of Latin Music from Bossa Nova to Salsa and Beyond* (Cambridge, MA: Da Capro Press, 2003), (xxi).
5. Morales, 13.

6. Jo Baim, *Tango: Creation of a Cultural Icon* (Bloomington and Indianapolis, IN: Indiana University Press, 2007), 133–139.

7. Martie Fellom, "Spain: Social and Theatrical Dance, 1700–1862," In Selma Jeanne Cohen, Ed. *International Encyclopedia of Dance*, Vol. 5 (New York: Oxford University Press, 1999), 605.

8. Lawrence Senelick, "Vaudeville Dance," In Selma Jeanne Cohen, Ed. *International Encyclopedia of Dance*, Vol. 6 (New York: Oxford University Press, 1999), 315–320.

9. Katarina Hazzard-Gordon, *Jookin': The Rise of Social Dance Formations in African-American Culture* (Philadelphia, PA: Temple University Press, 1990), 19, 67, 87.

10. http://sharlot.org/archives/history/dayspast/days_show.pl?name=2007 _04_15&h=%3Eelks%20theater%3E (accessed: June 12, 2010).

11. Senelick, 315–320.

12. Senelick, 315–320.

13. Ted Shawn, *One Thousand and One Night Stands* (Da Capro Press, Cambridge, MA: June 1979), 21.

14. Suzanne Shelton, *Divine Dancer: A Biography of Ruth St. Denis* (New York: Doubleday & Company, Inc., 1981) 121, and Ted Shawn, *One Thousand and One Night Stands*.

15. Fellom, 605.

16. Jonas, Shelton, et. al.

17. Cohen-Stratyner, Barbara. "The Franchising of Denishawn." *Dance Data* (no. 2), NY: 1977 (15–23).

18. Linda Tomko, *Dancing Class: Gender, Ethnicity, and Social Divides in American Dance, 1890–1920* (Bloomington and Indianapolis, IN: Indiana University Press, 1999), 22).

19. Jo Baim, *Tango: Creation of a Cultural Icon* (Bloomington and Indianapolis, IN: Indiana University Press, 2007), 66-67.

20. Jonas, 174.

21. Jonas, 175.

22. http://www.fredastaire.com/ Fredastairestudios.com (accessed: May 3, 2010).

23. Harry M. Benshoff and Sean Griffin, *America on Film: Representing Race, Class, Gender and Sexuality at the Movies* (Malden, MA: Blackwell Publishing, 2007), 140.

24. Sue Steward, *¡Musica! The Rhythm of Latin America: Salsa, Rumba, Merengue, and More* (San Francisco, CA: Chronicle Books, 1999), 31.

25. Benshoff and Griffin, 140–141.

26. http://www.imdb.com/title/tt0058725/ (accessed: February 2, 2010).

27. Henry Adaso, About.com Guide http://rap.about.com/od/breakdancing 101/p/Breakdancing.htm (accessed: July 3, 2010).

28. http://www.capoeirista.com/history (accessed: June 12, 2010).

29. Maria José Somerlate Barbosa,"Representation of Women in Capoeira Songs," Shayna McHugh, Trans. March 2008. http://www.plcs.umassd.edu/ plcs12texts/barbosajun162006.doc (accessed: April 8, 2010).

30. Matthias Röhrig Assunção, *Capoiera: a history of an Afro-Brazilian martial Art* (New York: Routledge, 2005) 109, 112.

31. http://www.virtualcapoeira.com/basics.htm (accessed: April 12, 2010).

Conclusion

El Triunfo's social chronicler reported in 1882 that Faíde's drummer "did everything but stand on his head" and sometimes "came apart bone by bone." The horrified writer [of a 1800s Havana women's magazine] imagined a future in which "Valenzuela's orchestra does away with all instruments except drums."[1]

Imagining the future of Latin social dance is a daunting idea. It is comforting to think that Latin dance and music will continue to inform social dancing in the United States as we pull round as of this writing into the 2010s decade and beyond. There are trends at work in our society into which Latin dance and music could well fit, based on how they have managed in the past to simultaneously remain relevant to the new and faithful to their fundamental identities. While the exact shape and direction of those fits can't be known, the flexibility and continual revision of relevancy to young and future dancers and musicians may give these kinds of dances the edge; after all, if Latin dancing can survive and thrive through the oppressions of slavery (of African-Americans) forced deportation (as in the case of the Arcadians) and immigration (Cubans, Puerto Ricans, Haitians, and Dominicans), then it is probably tough enough to move dancers through just about anything.

But what will these dances look like? One clue may lie in the very relationship between Latin dancing and music that allows an astonishing range of dances—South, Central, and Caribbean American—to fit with Latin jazz in the United States. So flexible is this relationship that

Mongo Santamaria in performance at New York's Blue Note Jazz Club, 1998.
(© Allen Spatz. Reprinted with permission.)

when the music starts, almost any style of Latin dancing can break out on the dance floor; one couple might step out with a sweet merengue shoulder-to-shoulder with another couple in a cha-cha. Or, unpartnered individuals perform bomba en masse, as a conga line waves around the perimeter of the dance floor, enclosing the event with celebration and communal joy. And if asked what it is they are dancing, everyone says, "Salsa!"

While many Latin dance enthusiasts conflate a variety of tropical dances under salsa, others make specific distinctions of the dances that go into what makes salsa. Still others describe salsa as one among other distinct and separate Latin dances. Denise Barnes, in her *Washington Times* article of September 12, 1996, "Oh, to Dance: Quite a Feat Classes Tap to the Beat, from Mambo to Modern" interviewed mambo instructor Byers on the issues of Latin music and dance. Byers stated that a historical awareness of both music and dance is absolutely crucial to really learning Latin social dances, how they fit together and with music, even though "Latin music is probably among the least understood of the popular music styles." Every dance has its own distinctive mood that picks up from the music: "the mambo is intense and steamy; the rumba is slow and romantic; the cha-cha is playful and seductive."[2]

But salsa is also described as one among several Latin dances, rather than a culmination of them:

> Each Latin dance cumbia, reggaeton and salsa, just to name a few gets your body pumping in different, unique ways while still giving you a sweat-infused workout. Cumbia focuses mainly on one side of your hips, and reggaeton is a high-intensity cardio workout, while salsa dancing works your stamina and leg strength. The rhythm for each routine changes from slow to fast depending on the song and dance.[3]

There is not, it would seem, anything like a uniform way of describing the relationship. Then, there is the question of what the dance and the music that goes with it is supposed to do; what its essential nature is designed to provide. What tango do we mean when we tango? Do we say that: "Tango is considered a 'walker's dance,' a glide, which has more to do with improvised footwork and less with choreographed steps. In other words, it doesn't have a competitive bone in it."[4]? Or, by tango do we mean the head-snapping, ballroom gown-and-tux version for DanceSport competition that is strictly choreographed and judged?

Another closely-related feature of Latin dances that indicates their future is that Latin dances so easily combine with other social dance forms without losing their own unique touch on the dance floor. It doesn't really matter where you're from, or how you got here, but while you're here, you can dance Latin. The dance and music has, throughout past development, drawn upon a mixture of sources: Amerindian, European, African, and Spanish (which has in itself North African, Islamic, and European notes). So that bridge between the familiar and the unfamiliar that helped Latin dancing become so popular in all sectors of U. S. culture in the past continues to bring new dancers to its style.

And if you need it, there is always someone close by to help you get that five-count clave beat lined up with your feet, arms, and hips. For example, Erin Boyt, who originally took dance training in Springfield, Missouri, describes her informal introduction to Latin dancing as tangential—yet supportive of—blues, swing, and modern. Using her skill in these other dances, she was quickly able to pick up Latin dancing through the best teacher of all—stepping out on the dance floor and just doing it. She said:

> I just learned to follow salsa. I remember once, I went to a dance in Springfield. My only experience with social dance at the time was swing, but one of my dance partners asked me if I knew cha-cha. I said no, but he said "That's okay! I'll show you!" He flung me around the dance floor with reckless abandon! It was the best time I'd had dancing in my entire life up to that point! He did, literally "show" me the cha-cha. Didn't say a single word through the whole dance, but he was so communicative with his body that I seemed to instinctually know just what to do.[5]

At the same time, there are limits to how far dancers can go in bending the dances to their desires. The salsa entry for Sonny Watson's website (which has the ambitious goal of cataloging all the dances and dancers who ever were, all over the world) points out that histories of dance origins become important as a matter of respect. In the past, Latin dances have been casually treated, especially as the pre-Castro Cuban tourist trade allowed just about anything that looked like a tropical Latin dance to be labeled "rumba." There was in this curious phenomenon certainly a fundamental economic, class, and racial bias, as Afro-Cuban dances in their original form were banned, but their "tamed down" versions pleased white tourists—who usually never encountered the original. To make matters more complicated, would-be teachers and exhibition dancers rushed to cash in on the demand, creating entirely different dances than those originally called "rumba," "cha-cha," or "samba."

While this effect has ended up enriching the range of Latin dances in the long run, it would be appropriate for contemporary Latin dancers and musicians to have a better appreciation of where things come from today. Dancing "salsa" with figures taken from a lindy or hip-hop as tricks might not quite fit the musical phrasing, and it shows—badly—on the dancers. While some merges between dances can work, the feel of it clicks only if the dancers keep track of what's what. And, "there are some great male and female Latin dancers out there doing truly amazing feet rhythms and body movements that sizzle and flow with the music and who have 'real style' rather than 'tricks,' and yes, you know who they are when you see them."[6]

Latin dancers today also have other interests related to dancing. Allowing the dance to inform the non-dance activity, and vice versa, presents no obstacle whatsoever. It seems reasonable that this trend would continue, suggesting a continuation of more style fusions than separations, perhaps a reflection of a global community made instantly accessible through the Internet. I recently interviewed the Seattle club dancer Pablos Holman on his habits in Latin dancing related to other kinds of movement skills:

> I'd been practicing Aikido (a Japanese marital art) for about a decade, and one night I saw some exceptional tango dancers perform. They had mastered a physical communication that we practice in Aikido. I took some lessons from them, but quickly discovered that tango required more structure and discipline than I had to offer. I switched to salsa and it was a much better fit for me. Now I get to explore the same fundamentals as Aikido, but instead of practicing with sweaty old Japanese guys, I get to practice with sweaty young Latin girls![7]

Then there is the way that Latin dances whisper a new and ever-changing fascination to each succeeding generation of dancers, indicating that they are not apt to vanish from the social dance floors of the United States anytime soon. Not only is Latin dancing available in every major city, but throughout the United States. If there isn't a specifically designated Latin dance club in town, it is still pretty likely that there are at least a couple of zumba dance exercise programs going on at the local YMCA. Holman has no trouble at all taking his Latin dancing with him everywhere he goes, and has enjoyed checking out the Latin spots in any town he gets to. But he also said he was glad to get back to Seattle because:

> We have a great dance community and I like dancing with people I've gotten to know. I'm mostly an "On1" salsa and bachata dancer. I am also in blues dancing, which isn't strictly Latin, but it looks that way when I do it! I dance four or five nights a week these days; that probably qualifies as a mild obsession. There is salsa somewhere in Seattle every night of the week (e.g., Century Ballroom, SeeSound Lounge, Triple Door, Babalu, El Malecon).[8]

Even the most isolated previous styles are coming forward in unexpected places. Cajun, zydeco, and tejano developed more or less regionally and linguistically isolated from mainstream commercial pop culture of the United States. By the time they entered the professional media market, they had adapted to the new millennium with firm connections to their original foundations. Homegrown and relevant to humble, working-class dancers and musicians, these dances developed through small neighborhood and family parties, rather than in urban professional venues. They invoke a nostalgic desire, reflected in the close holds of the dancers, for simple rural values and the joys and sorrows of the displaced immigrant that resonate with folks growing up far from Louisiana and the Southwest.

These music and dance traditions also struggled to survive class and ethnic discrimination. At one time, youngsters keen to fit into the mainstream culture looked down on these "old folks" styles of dance and music. And it had as much to do with language as with culture; during the 1940s and 1950s, public education policy attempted to force abandonment of all languages except English. Youngsters were ashamed of their ethnic heritage, which separated them from the mainstream culture. But dedicated musicians who fostered unique dance and music traditions in French (Cajun and zydeco) and Mexican Spanish (tejano) were able, through extensive touring of their bands and by cutting recordings, to bring the music into wider public notice and popularity. And Spanish-language based media and recording companies fed a resurgence of identity sometimes called "reverse assimilation," in which bilingual grandchildren communicate with, and relate to, their own grandparents better than their parents could.[9]

Keeping track of those roots and the way they sustain the future is what keeps Mitchell Marks, who started dancing as a boy, firmly connected to Latin dance in his own multiracial heritage. Although he is speaking of salsa, the same kind of determined survival shines through his words on a par to the survival of Cajun and zydeco. He said:

> I was more of a watcher than anything. I was a very shy child, but salsa made me feel so real, to this day there is no other emotion I've known that makes me feel so here in my flesh! There are numerous clubs in Seattle that play great salsa; there is a salsa night at the Triple Door. There is China Harbor, El Malecon, Rock Salt, and numerous other locations. The music is so much deeper than words—there is no amount of words to speak to convey my greatest recognition of what was before and after. My heart goes so far into what was before, because that is where I am every time I hear the sounds of salsa.[10]

Although some fear that zydeco is disappearing into senior centers because the young people prefer more media-driven music and dance, evidence suggests there is a resurgence of interest in zydeco as far away as Oregon, with the likes of Portland's Bon Ton Roulet band. And the Eugene Zydeco Dance Community invites one and all to "come dance to the sweet and the hot" every second Wednesday of the month at the New Day Bakery and World Café.[11]

Today, Cajun, zydeco, and tejano make a stand in urban dance clubs right along with salsa and other Latin dances all over the United States and abroad as part of the rich legacy of a multicultural and multilingual society. And maybe—probably—the Latin dance floor will be around for many more to enjoy. But is it the real, "authentic" Cajun and zydeco dance and music they're doing in Oregon? What happens when this tradition gets moved from a rural to an urban setting—say, from the small communities of East Texas to New Orleans; is it still the same? For that matter, should it be the same? Or, should the test of its relevancy continue as it began when the original Arcadians left Canada for Louisiana, taking their dance and music with them? Only time will tell. Let new generations of dancers take up Latin dances and make of them what they will. In the meantime, it is up to those dancing now to continue to discover what it is in Latin dance that compels them to return and return again, making the style, the beat of the drum, part of who they are and wish to be.

Notes

1. John Charles Chasteen, *National Rhythms, African Roots: The Deep History of Latin American Popular Dance* (Albuquerque, NM: University of New Mexico Press, 2004), 79.

2. Denise Barnes, "Oh, to Dance: Quite a Feat Classes Tap to the Beat, from Mambo to Modern," *The Washington Times*, September 12, 1996, 4, http://www.questia.com/PM.qst?a=o&d=5000472455. (accessed: April 10, 2010).

3. Jennifer Rundell, "Let's Zumba," *Daily Herald* (Arlington Heights, IL), September 1, 2008, http://www.questia.com/PM.qst?a=o&d=5033795206 (accessed: April 10, 2010).

4. "Embrace the Music and Your Partner; Tango's Sexy Form Glides onto D.C. Scene," *The Washington Times*, March 21, 2002, M10, http://www.questia.com/PM.qst?a=o&d=5000721252 (accessed: August 12, 2010).

5. Author interview with Erin Boyt, April 14, 2010

6. Sonny Watson's Streetswing.com www.Archives streetswing.com/histmain/d5index.htm (accessed August 8, 2009).

7. Author interview with Pablos Holman, April 11, 2010.

8. Author interview with Pablos Holman, April 11, 2010.

9. Author journal record interview of retired teacher Guadelupe Baca-Vaughn, Taos, NM 1976.

10. Author interview with Mitchell Marks, April 27, 2010.

11. http://www.myspace.com/eugenezydeco (accessed March 5, 2010).

Appendix I

Online Resources

General Latin Dance

YouTube.com	(keyword the dance style)
Planetnightlife.com	links to info sites by city
www.dancecrazy.com/LatinDanceSteps	
vidasalsera.com	Salsa clubs in Los Angeles
salsaweb.com	
mejordecuba.com	Salsa clubs in New York City
latinclubs.com	+ mambo
www.salsanewyork.com	general directory
latin-dance.net	
clubmayan.com	South Carolina
charlestonsalsaclub.com	+ area festivals

Cajun/Zydeco

cajunzydeco.net	Cajun and zydeco resources
zydecodowntown.com	
buckwheatzydeco.com	
zydeco.org	
zydecoevents.com	

Capoeira/Breaking

capoeirista.com	
capoeira.com	
planetcapoeira.com	
breakdance.com	
rap.about.com/od/breakdancing101	
www.breakdanceclass.com	instruction demonstrations
essortment.com	history

Ballroom Latin Dance/Instruction
BallRoomDance101.com
arthurmurray.com
fredastaire.com
ballroomdancers.com   DanceSport competition
dancevision.com   ballroom dance camp
usaballroomdance.org

Tango
continentaldanceclub.com
ridance.com/ritango

Zumba
zumba.com   zumba exercise classes

Wheelchair Ballroom
www.wheelchairdancesportusa.org
groovability.org

Appendix II

Latin Dance on Film

Spanish Latin Dances

1919	Rogue's Romance	tango/maxixie
1921	The Four Horsemen of the Apocalypse	tango/maxixie
1922	Blood and Sand	tango/maxixie
1935	Noches de Buenos Aires	tango
1940	The Mark of Zorro	generic Spanish
1944	Knickerbocker Holiday	flamenco/bolero
1945	Los amores de un torero	
1946	La noche y tú	tango
1949	The Story of the Tango	
1961	Alias Gardelito	tango/music
1963	Los Tarantos	tango
1972	Ultimo tango a Parigi	
1982	Starstruck	tango/other
1992	Tango Argentino	
1992	Scent of a Woman	tango
1992	Strictly Ballroom	paso doble
1993	Tango feroz: la leyenda de Tanguito	
1993	Tango	
1996	Shall We Dance? (Japan)	tango
1997	The Tango Lesson	
1999	Flawless	tango
2000	Malèna	tango
2002	Frieda	tango
2003	Tango Bar	
2004	Shall We Dance? (USA)	tango
2006	Take The Lead	tango

Breaking and Capoeira

1982	Style Wars (PBS documentary)

1983	Wild Style
1983	Flashdance
1984	Beat Street
1984	Breakin'
1984	Breakin' 2 Electric Boogaloo
1985	Delivery Boys
1985	Krush Groove
1985	Break Boy
1989	Rooftops
1993	Only the Strong
1998	Blade
2001	Zoolander
2002	The Freshest Kids: A History of the B-Boy
2007	Planet B-Boy
2007	Ó Paí, Ó

Zyceco, Cajun, and Tejano?

1973	Hot Pepper (documentary on Clifton Chernier)	zydeco
1993	Louisiana Blues	
1997	Selena	
2000	Rhythm 'n' Bayous: A Road Map to Louisiana Music	documentary
2003	Schultze Gets the Blues	zydeco

Tropical Latin and Salsa

1933	A Voz do Carnaval	
1935	Alô, Alô, Brasil	samba
1937	A Day at the Races	Lindy
1950	Musica, Mujeres y piratas	
1956	And God Created Woman	mambo
1959	Black Orpheus	samba/bossa nova
1975	Queen of the Stardust Ballroom	
1977	Saturday Night Fever	disco
1987	Dirty Dancing	mambo/freestyle
1990	Lambada	
1992	Mambo Kings	
1995	Manhattan Merengue!	
1998	Dance With Me	salsa
2000	Mad about Mambo	
2005	Mad Hot Ballroom	rumba/merengue
2010	Non-stop to Brazil	bossa nova

Hollywood Good Neighbor Films with Latin Dances

1933	Flying Down to Rio	samba/carioca
1940	Down Argentine Way	
1941	Week-End in Havana	
1941	That Night in Rio	

1942	Rhumba Rhythms	
1942	Panama Hattie	
1944	Something for the Boys	samba boogie
1946	Cuban Pete	mambo/other
1947	Copacabana	
1995	Carmen Miranda: Bananas Is My Business	
2008	Carmen Miranda: That Girl from Rio	

Glossary

Apanpichao: The third section of a merengue dance piece performed in swing rhythm.

Apito or Pito: An extremely penetrating, high-pitched, three-note "pea" whistle indispensable as the starting signal for Brazilian samba processionals. The whistle keeps up a sharp quality to the beat throughout the set, signaling sequence changes. However, in recent times the apito has made an appearance in other Latin social dances. Adept fingering over the side chamber holes in different configurations produces three different tones.

Bajo sexto: Twelve-string guitar essential as the bass and harmonic complement to the melody of the accordion for a conjunto ensemble.

Bandoneon: A button accordion originally from Germany; indispensable for traditional tango music.

Batá: An African-styled drum essential to sacred Afro-Cuban Santería rituals, the batá is a "talking or singing" drum shaped like an hourglass. The leather straps binding the batá have beads and bells attached that sound as the drum is moved. When the straps are pulled or loosened by the musician, the pitch of the drum can be very rapidly changed, not unlike a singing voice. Batá are sacred objects kept wrapped in a cloth the color of the Orisha to which each particular drum is dedicated; for example, the Orisha Chango associated with St. Barbara in red and white finds his voice through this drum. Traditionally, only men played them, but recently all-women batá groups perform. The secretive Abakwa religion's holiest drum, the ekue, is never seen, but played from behind a curtain.[1]

Batuque: Basis of the Brazilian samba in both its couples and processional forms, as well as capoeira: a kind of dance/game/ritual of Cape Verde performed in lines or circles as individuals take turns free-styling to the music.

Beguine: Set in 4/4 time, the beguine is something like a slow and sultry rumba introduced from the West Indies (beguine is feminine form of the word "begue," or "white person") into the United States in the 1920s. Although briefly popular in the 1930s, the dance didn't catch on; the song, *Begin the Beguine* (1935) by Cole Porter (1892–1964) was featured in the Fred Astaire/Eleanor Powell movie *Broadway Melody of 1940* (MGM, 1940).

Bells: Two main types are the agogô and a clapperless cowbell (also called the cencerro), both of which keep a constant base rhythmic beat throughout the piece. Like the cowbell, agogôs were held together in one hand, and struck by the other with a small wooden or metal rod. Later, the bells were mounted on a stand.

Berimbau: A single-string Brazilian musical bow with a hollowed gourd resonator originating in Africa and brought with slaves into South America. Similar African instruments have been played since prehistoric times, and it is now widely accepted as having originated in Angola. The bow is held in the left hand in which a stone or coin is also held pressed against the string to produce tone variations in pitch or even a buzzing sound. The string is played with a thin stick and held in the right hand, which also holds a basket shaker known as a caxixi. Opening and closing the gourd also alters the pitch of the instrument.

Bola: A fairly vigorous new dance in Cuba.

Bongos: Two small, shallow Afro-Cuban drums permanently attached to each other. The larger bongo is tuned about fifth below the smaller one. Bongos are widely used in the popular music of Latin America and in U.S. dance scenes featuring most styles of Latin and Latin-influenced dancing; in the 1950s, bongôs were a counterculture symbol of the beatniks.

Boteo: 1960s Cuban dance music.

Cajon or Cajas: Literally, a hollow wooden box played in the Afro-Cuban Rumba Yambú, but also in other tropical Latin dance/music. The box is played by striking the sides with the hand or with a wooden mallet.

Cajun: Strictly speaking, the term refers to French Canadians (Arcadians) and their descendants who settled in the Western Louisiana region. Cajun dance traditionally includes a two-step, waltz, and jig.[4] But the music and French lyrics of Cajun contribute to the richness of zydeco.

Calypso: Afro-Carib music, a combination of slave and French Creole elements; originally from Trinidad and Tobago. Calypso musicians compete during Carnival.

Candombe: Montevideo carnival music.

Carioca: A swaying group dance to samba beat named for the Carioca (a Tupi Indian word for "white house") River of Rio de Janiero, Brazil. As a couples dance, partners touch foreheads while dancing, as featured in the Fred Astaire/Ginger Rogers (MGM, 1933) movie, *Flying Down to Rio*.[2] Carioca also refers to a belly dance and a lambada-style 1990s Cuban couples dance similar to a despelote.

Casino: A contemporary Cuban version of salsa; fast and sassy. A rueda (wheel) de casino dance is one in which an exchange of partners is called out by the vocalist among four or more pairs in a circle, and some of the figures resemble Western square dancing. The dance is currently popular in Cuba.[3]

Castanets: Held either in the hands of the dancer or a musician, castanets are paired clam-shell-shaped instruments that fit loosely

A close-up of the hands of a dancer playing the castanets. (© Rami Katzav/ iStockPhoto.com.)

within the palms. They are played by striking the thick rim of two halves together for a sharp, commanding sound. A castanet "roll" is a five-strike sequence similar to clave.

Charanga: Cuban danzón band, one kind of orquesta típicas which has been made lighter and faster-paced in its playing by eliminating the brass and using flutes, violins, and piano.[5]

Clave: Refers to the fundamental rhythmic "Latin beat" distinct from though closely related to jazz. Clave also refers to the musical instrument that keeps that beat consistent for musicians and dancers. The Afro-Cuban percussion instrument claves consists of two wooden sticks about seven inches long and one inch in diameter made of rosewood, ebony, or genadillo. To play the claves, the musician holds one stick in each hand and strikes them against each other. A "clave rhythm" is a five-strike pattern that can be performed as a "forward" (Cuban "son" clave) of three notes followed by two, or as a "reversed" ("African" or "rumba" clave) of two notes followed by three.

Colombia: A fast and acrobatic rumba brave dance performed by men.

Comparsa: Grouping of musicians, singers, and dancers for a carnival.

Conga: A conga is both a serpentine line dance of Afro-Cuban origin and the single-headed drum that is part of the accompaniment. The distinctive shape of a conga drum is achieved by a wooden shell that bulges in the middle. Like many drums in the Latin group, Congas are usually played with the hands to produce a variety of percussive pitches and tones.

Contrary Move: Difficult to describe in words, this dance gesture is: "the action of turning the opposite hip and shoulder toward the direction of the moving leg and is used to commence all turning movements that occurs frequently in the tango."[6] This moving position, in which the leg is placed across the body, is also a feature of other Spanish classical and folk dances as well as in ballet and fencing. The line of the body is sometimes described as a "closed" position preliminary to an outside turn that will once again present an "open" body profile when completed. In a pause, a contrary movement presents the spectator with a sculptural view of the dancing body.

Corrido: A narrative folk ballad style of Mexican origin developed by tejanos (Tex/Mex).

Corté: The word in Spanish means "cut," and it involves a stop before a change of direction forward or backward. The corté step specifically characterizes the tango so strongly that when applied to other dances, it has the effect of making them into tangos; the tango is also referred to as, "baile con corté" ("dance with a stop").[7] Tango choreography is referred to as "corte y quebrada" (stop and break). The corté is an example of how the rhythmic structure and style of movements make a Latin dance more clearly a matter of a combination of features above and beyond the name it has been given or the music played to accompany it.

Creole: Former African slaves or Hatian refugees and their descendants who settled in and around the West Louisiana area to exchange language, music, and dance with the Cajun. Zydeco is a Creole dance and music style sung in French, yet a distinctively African-American form.

Criollo: Technically, criollo refers to Spanish colonials regardless of racial or ethnic background, or whites and their descendants who have settled in the Americas. In the Dominican Republic, the term criollo refers to something made in Spain, as opposed to something home-made or of Afro-Dominican origin.[8]

Cuatro: A doubled five-string instrument sometimes used in salsa bands.

Cuban motion: Also called "Latin motion," the gesture is anything from a demure hip movement to an expressly aggressive pelvic rotation achieved by alternately bending and straightening each knee one after the other in such a way as to sway the hips from side to side combined with a "lateral movement of hips and ribcage."[9] It is also a "break" in the vertical line of the body (quebrar or requebrar).[10] The precise weight transfer of the dancers' bodies is usually held well tucked under, so that each step is very small and dancing couples can spot dance on a crowded floor. A good Cuban motion is an important element of such tropical Latin dances as salsa, rumba, mambo, cha-cha, and merengue.

Cubop: A 1940s Latin jazz fusion between Cuban and bebop.

Cuddle: An open hold side-by-side position in which the man stands to the right and the woman to the left, holding hands with arms entwined and facing the same direction. Partners hold proximal hands together with the man's left arm over his partner's shoulder, while her right arm crosses his chest. The position allows for rapid turns in either direction while partners retain close contact. More often seen in swing dances, the cuddle sometimes makes an appearance in Latin/ Jazz hybrids such as a salsa.

Cuerpo: The "body" of a merengue central section that sets up the melody.

Cuica: A friction drum from Brazil often played to accompany samba, the cuica is toned by a stick fixed in the center of the drum skin and projects from inside the shell. The sound is made by rubbing the stick between the thumb and the forefinger with a damp sponge or piece of leather.

Cumbia: Originally a Colombian music and dance style, cumbia fuses Spanish, African, and indigenous musical traditions with European popular music. It became part of Colombia's independence movement and cultural push toward nationalism in the 1920s.

Danzón: Late 1800s Afro-Cuban ballroom dance influenced by European styles played by charangas.[11] Danzón also refers to Cuban bands that play traditional cha-cha rhythms featuring violins, flute, and percussion.

Desafío: The challenge essential to rumba brava.

Descarga: Improvised section of tropical Latin music featuring individual instruments or a dialogue between instruments (between horns and percussion). Traditional salsas feature a descarga during the middle to the end of the piece in which the coro (backup singers) or vocal section that repeats a phrase over and over above the descarga improvises. Here the singer may, off the top of his/her head talk about the issues of the day, another band member, or anything else the vocalist may deem important. The descarga can happen within a formal or informal setting.[12]

Diabolitos: "Little devils," heavily masked and costumed dancers of the abakwa religion who bring the gods into life. "Diablo" was a 1940s rhythm leading to the mambo.

Escolas de Samba: "Schools" or club groups of Rio samba carnival musicians, singers, and dancers—first established in the 1920s and continuing to the present day.

Fan: The word refers to a dance move and a musical section. The fan in dance terms is a half-turn on the ball of the foot, with the free foot held behind it, one of the eight basic and most distinctive moves of a tango, and evidence of its strong Spanish association. In Latin musical terms, the "fan" (abancio) is played on the timbales drums, particularly for a salsa. Its purpose is to "open and close" specific musical sections that are either improvised or set.

Fandango: Meaning "go and dance," a Spanish courtship dance probably originating in Moorish Andalusia as a fairly racy version of flamenco despite the fact that partners do not touch—ancestor to the bolero.

Fervo: From "fever," or "to boil," military brass band "call and response" music of 1800s Brazil for maxixie, two-step, and polka; it is the basis of music for capoeira.

Frottoir: The washboard adapted to Zydeco music; a piece of corrugated metal worn on the chest of the musician and scraped with spoons or aluminum can openers.[13]

Guaguancó: One form of rumba brava dance featuring a pelvic thrust.

Guaracha: A medium-tempo satiric song and dance style originating in Spain, where it most closely resembled a bolero. Around the 1850s, the guaracha that had been popular in Cuba moved into Puerto Rican jíbaro dances.

Habanera: A type of 2/4 Cuban dance music evolved from the danzón/contradance ballroom styles that got its name after it left Cuba and became popular in the United States and Mexico around the turn of the century. The repeating five-count rhythm of a habanera was reputedly brought into the United States by the New Orleans composer/musician Louis Moreau Gottschalk, at which point it was called the "tango bass." Habanera rhythm also hit Buenos Aires and was absorbed into the tango.[14]

Hestitation: The hesitation is "a figure or part of a figure in which progression is temporarily suspended, and the weight retained on one foot for more than one count." A hover kind of hesitation is "a part of a figure in which the moving or turning of the body is checked, while the feet remain almost stationary."[15] Often, the hesitation is part of a Spanish Latin dance like the tango, paso doble, or a bolero and the only time in which dancers may rise to the balls of the feet to signal a change of locomotive direction.

Holds: Holds describe how dance partners move together. In social dances there are two basic types of holds; open and closed. Holds are as important to all Latin dances as to other social dances. An open hold means that the partners are holding hands and can move toward or away from each other while still maintaining this minimal physical contact. A closed hold means that both partners face each other in an embrace that may (or may not) include full or partial torso contact.

Huapango: A lively dance that originated along the Mexican gulf coast that contributed to Conjunto/Tejano—a distortion of a habanera.

Jala jala: A carnival conga rhythm adapted to U.S. Latin and other popular dances in the 1960s.

Jaleo: Fast-paced instrumental refrain section of a merengue.

Jíbaro: Literally, "those who escape civilization"; refers to the mix of Spanish and mulatto peasants and escaped slaves who formed their own autonomous, ethnic-relative socio-political orders, or cabildos. "Both guajiros [Cuban sharecroppers] and [Puerto Rican] jíbaros share many features with the bluesmen of the American South and the poor whites who created U.S. country and western music."[16]

Laina: Lead singer in a plena of Puerto Rico who improvises commentary, satire, and leads the figures of a modern bomba dance.

La-la: What zydeco music was called before the term "zydeco" was commonly accepted and used for this style of music.

Lead/Follow: When two people dance closely together, one must lead and the other must follow. As the man and woman face one another in a couple hold, the man leads by stepping forward on his right foot, while the woman follows by correspondingly stepping backward on her left.

Lundú: Bantu and Angolan music and dance style from which the samba is derived. Lundú is also a type of polka that contributed to the maxixie.

Marimba: A lot like a xylophone but somewhat smaller, marimbas are an Afro-Brazilian percussion instrument essential to any traditional tropical Latin dance band. Marimbas have a soft, mellow tone because the keys are made of rosewood with brass or aluminum resonators; however, the need to project over a full compliment of musical instruments in a large modern orchestra calls for the all-metallic xylophone. Sometimes the Marimba is given its own improvisational section. A marimbula is a small version of a marimba that can be hand-held for a traditional merengue musician.

Mestizo: Spanish for mixed European and indigenous blood.

Milonga: A song and dance style of the late 1800s, milonga is tied to the development of the Argentine tango. The term also refers to places where people go to learn and to dance the tango, or the song lyrics sung by payadores.

Mina: The betraying woman of tango.

Moña: Horn section patterns often written, but sometimes improvised. The moñero is the musician adept at developing rich and interesting moñas.

Montuno: The repetition call and response section of a Latin dance song sung by vocalists is referred to as the montuno. It is often mistaken for a specific type rhythm or song form, but actually refers to the African tradition of call/response in both secular and sacred events. The dance done during this part of the music also became known as the mambo (see Son).

Mulata: Women whose skin color is between black and white; attractive mulatas are featured on the floats where they perform a variation of samba during Carnival time in Brazil. The ability of a mulata to perfect an astonishing variety of hip and pelvic moves in her dance is highly-prized and her lavishly colorful, yet skimpy costume is a reminder that all things of the flesh are to be enjoyed during Carnival before the season of Lent begins.

Música Tropical: A recent music combination of cumbia in so-called "turbo conjuntos" with country and pop-rock; singer Selena was a stellar exponent of the pop-rock/cumbia merger.[17]

Nueva Canción: Literally meaning "new song," this song music style is a Cuban/Argentine hybrid that made its appearance during the mid 1970s. Part of the Nuyorican (Puerto Rican culture in New York City) scene, Nueva Canción and the Golden Age of Salsa did not enter the mainstream of U. S. social dance (Salsa would become popular in that venue about ten years later), but remained strong in the South Bronx and East Harlem. This intensely North American Latin style may have had some degree of influence on neighboring NYC musical genres like hip-hop, house, and freestyle dance music. However, it also shows itself in the works of socially-conscious Salsa lyrics writers such as Rubén Blades.[18]

Nuyorican: This is a "Spanglish" term melding New York and Puerto Rican culture. Nuyorican dance and music continues to evolve and change through the added textures of new populations into a generalized (that is, not just Puerto Rican) Latin North American urban scene.

Orquesta Tajana: A dance music ensemble of the Tex/Mex genre; the music, which appealed to the middle class in contrast to conjunto (which appealed to the working poor). Orquesta Tejana made a leap into the North American urban mainstream with ranchero-based music in the late 1940s, and incorporated Afro-Hispanic rhythms to keep up with other modern Latin-styled big dance bands of the era. Their sound is referred to as "jaitón" (from the English "high-toned").[19]

Pachanga: Originally a Cuban rural festival dance (the name means "Cuban dance party") and music style, sometimes identified as a charanga, with which it is generally interchangeable. Music for this fast dance was a hybrid between merengue and conga (merenconga). Although pachanga replaced the cha-cha and was briefly popular in Cuba and the United States in the 1960s, it did not endure.[20]

Pambiche: Santo Domingo dance briefly popular in the Dominican Republic during the U. S. occupation.

Pandeiro: This rhythm percussion instrument is a lot like a tambourine. The basic design of a small frame drum with metal jingles around the circumference is the same; however, a pandeiro is usually larger in size. The other important difference is in the jingles. The modern orchestral tambourine has been developed to produce a "brilliant" sound to cut easily though an orchestra, so the jingles are made of a hard metal like steel or brass. Pandeiro jingles are more often made of softer tin like the original "bottle-top jingles," and therefore produce a much drier sound that is more suited to the fast rhythms of Brazilian music such as samba.[21]

Panderos: Tambourine essential to traditional Puerto Rican plena music without bells. They are usually played in three sizes; the largest and medium ones keep the beat, while the smallest improvises.

Payadores: Itinerant and illiterate peasant singers whose songs adopted from gauchos' ballads were eventually incorporated into tango lyrics.[22]

Pendulum Motion: This move is one type of "isolation," or the ability of a dancer to move different parts of the body in different directions and with different rhythmic phrasing. A feature of most tropical Latin social dances, pendulum motion is part of the larger technique of isolations characteristic of African dance traditions and urban U. S. street dancing, as well as American modern concert dance. In a samba, pendulum motion is achieved when the dancer's upper body leans away from the locomotive direction of the steps taken by the feet.

Quebrada: A swiveling of the hips characteristic of Cuban folk dances, which found its way into the old-style milonga tango.

Ranchero: Style of Norteño music and dance for a country-styled waltz (vals ranchero) or polka (polca ranchera) rhythmic signature popular among Mexican Americans along the border in the late 1940s after Beto Villa recorded the first orquesta tejana sound under the Ideal label. Ranchero is also a Mexican style of balladic singing.

Reblieo: A samba gesture performed by the highly-sexualized float dancers during Carnival. The buttocks are pushed out and rolled in a circular motion, while the knees are well bent, and the feet planted apart. A distinctly Afro-Latin movement, the gesture is often found in MTV videos featuring rap, and a variation of it is a distinctive characteristic of reggaeton (which also features a Spanish rap lyric accompaniment).

Roda: The circle of open space created by the ring of participant/ observers in which capoeira partners perform.

Rumbas: Aside from the r(h)umba social dance, a "rumba" refers to an informal gathering of musicians combining African drumming and Spanish or African vocal traditions with improvised dancing and singing (also called "rumba brava"). In addition, a "rumba clave" beat (also called an "African" or "reverse clave") drives the pace and syncopation of the music.

Santería: Sometimes also referred to as regal de ocha. Afro-carib ceremonies (bembés, "blessings") in which the Orishas (or Yoruba deities) are summoned to speak through music and dance. A melding of Catholic saints with Yoruba ancestor/spirits, Santería entered the tourist trade in the lean years of the 1990s.

Scrapers: Latin dance music features a marvelous array of scrapers made of wood, gourd, metal (guiros), or thin-notched Brazilian bamboo. The surface of the scraper has been scored to make ridges, and the hollow frame also has holes cut into it by which the instrument is held, and which also texture the sound. Scrapers are played by raking reed or metal tines across the ridges, or variously they can also be tapped by the wooden handle into which the tines have been set. Perhaps the most unusual scraper of all is the quijano (quijada), the jawbone of a horse or donkey used in old-time Cuban music. The quijano is scraped with a stick so that the loose teeth in the jawbone make a rattling sound. This family of percussion instruments is collectively referred to as reco-reco.

Shakers: This family of different kinds of hand-held rattles comes in a dazzling array of shapes and sizes. Like many small Latin percussive musical instruments, shakers allow dancers to perform as musicians and vice versa. The most well-known of them used in Mexican, Cuban, and Puerto-Rican dance rhythms is the maracas, which come in pairs (one held by the handle in each hand). Other shakers include the chocalo and cabaça (made out of tin cans), and the cabassa and shekere (made out of gourds over which a netting with beads have been stretched). A chachá is a Hatian metal shaker adapted to Cuban music; some say its sound was like the shuffling of cha-cha dancers' feet and that it gave its name to the dance. A traditional rumba brava makes use of cucharas (spoons clacked together similar to castanets) and maranga, or iron rattle.

Shines: These "no hold/touch-free" couples social dance positions require no physical contact between partners even while they are dancing close together. Latin dances that include shines are salsa (in which an "open shine" signifies free-style improvisation), samba, and bossa nova (in which the shine may, as in a minuet, have each of the two partners turn in a circle away from each other before rejoining in a hold). Shines take a bit of practice to perform well, but provide a provocative, witty, and flirtatious note between partners.

Shing-a-ling: Latin-style dance popular in New York during the 1960s; something like the Boogaloo.

Son: One important form that establishes a bridge between African (former slaves) and Spanish (South American/Caribbean farmers, or campesinos) cultures, son (literally, sonido or "sound") is the root of most familiar styles of Afro-Cuban dance music. A son clave beat is a "forward" 3/2 rhythm. Son encouraged the inclusion of an improvisational break section (coro) in contemporary salsa.

Spot Dance: It is very important on a crowded social dance floor for couples to be able to move together in a small, confined space without colliding with other dancers. A spot dance is performed in a "claimed" space, and it is usually up to the gentleman to steer his partner away from collisions with other dancers. Good tropical Latin spot dances include the Dominican bachata/merengue, the steps of which do not depend upon the broad locomotion of a couple in order to achieve them. Spot dances do not make for the best DanceSport ballroom or exhibition dance styles, and vice versa.

Surdo: An essential instrument of Brazilian samba processions, the surdo is a large bass drum hung on a rope around the neck, so the head is flat and can be reached with both hands. The drum is played with a single large-headed mallet, while the other hand is employed to vary the sound by sometimes pressing on the head to create a slightly higher pitched "closed" or muffled sound.

Tacuachito: Literally meaning "possum," a style of Norteño polka that is danced very slowly in "a deliberate, swaying glide reminiscent of a pregnant possum."[23]

Tambora: Merengue double-head drum played with both hands, one striking with a stick.

Tamborim: Essential to Brazilian dances, the tamborim is a high-pitched hand-held frame drum struck with a stick or mallet (as opposed to most other Latin music drums played with the hands). Useful in creating counter rhythms to the lower tones of base-beat drums, tamborims yield two different pitches, depending on how the hand holding the drum is pressed against the skin of the drumhead from the inside.

Tembleque: Literally, tremble; the shaking vibration of a rumba brava dancer; sometimes in mambo.

Timbales: Also, paila in Cuba. Consisting of a pair of shallow drums with metal shells, timbales have skin heads on the top side only. When they are struck with thin wooden sticks, these drums produce an extremely sharp, staccato sound something like a kettledrum (which in French is "timbale"). Although they sound nothing at all like orchestral timpani, they share the same quality of sound. The timbales set up figures to open and closed musical sections called the abancio (fan). The cascara (meaning "shell") rhythm is played on the side of a timbale during salsa lyric verses and the softer sections. Timbales musicians often also play the cowbells in a typical Latin band.

Tres: A small guitar with three sets of doubled strings, the tres is a standard instrument for traditional Cuban music.

Triangle: Used in traditional Cajun music as well as modern Latin dance accompaniment. Brazilian samba triangles are bigger and coarser than orchestra triangles, and the sound they produce is "thicker." To play a samba pattern on a triangle, the musician needs to get an open and choked sound. The open sounds are used for the accents on the first and fourth semiquavers of each beat, following the chocalo pattern. Sometimes this pattern is reversed, so that the closed sound is used for the accents. The triangle is suspended on the bent index finger while the palm and other fingers can close or grip from here to choke the sound while the beater is used in a side-to-side motion inside the triangle.

Trova: The word is an echo of "troubadour" in that trovador musicians were itinerant, traveling the countryside and accompanying themselves on the guitar. "Nueva trova" refers to Cuban social issues songs of the 1960s.

Tumba: The Dominican national dance in Santo Domingo of the late 1800s; supplanted for its African connections by the merengue during Trujillo's dictatorship.

Vogueing: The art of the "iconic moment" in dance or performance movement designed to give a clear image of meaning for the camera's eye, most often in tango, but also in other exhibition Latin dances.

Yambú: A slow rumba brava.

Zouk: Meaning, "party," or possibly a variation of "juke." A recent "reincarnation" of the Lambada featuring extra hip movements (such as a "flick") for the woman dancing to zouk music. Sometimes called zouk-lambada. The music is eclectic, sometimes including Arabic rhythms, as well as R&B.

ZyDeCajun: An amalgam of zydeco and Cajun; song lyrics are in English and French, and the band often includes a modern drum set, piano, and electric guitar as well as more traditional instruments. Exponent Wayne Toups states that ZyDeCajun gets its vitality from an infusion of R & B and a little country and western.[24]

Notes

1. Sue Steward, ¡*Musica! The Rhythm of Latin America: Salsa, Rumba, Merengue, and More* (San Francisco, CA: Chronicle Books, 1999), 13.

2. Sonny Watson swingtime.com (accessed: March 19, 2010).

3. http://www.youtube.com/watch?v=FBktrYd7Ae8 a sample from boogalu .com (accessed: May 1, 2010).

4. http://www.cajundance.com/dances.htm (accessed: March 11, 2010).

5. Ed Morales, *The Latin Beat: The Rhythms and Roots of Latin Music from Bossa Nova to Salsa and Beyond* (Cambridge, MA: Da Capro Press, 2003), 12–13. And Isabelle Leymarie, *Cuban Fire: the Saga of Salsa and LatinJjazz* (London and New York: Continuum, 2002), 344.

6. Alex Moore, *Ballroom Dancing*. 10th Ed. (New York: Routledge, 2005), 15–17.

7. http://www.showgate.com (accessed: February 15, 2010).

8. From Author's unpublished Dominican Republic journal notes; 1979–82.

9. Yvonne Marceau, "Ballroom Dance Competition," In Selma Jeanne Cohen, Ed. *International Encyclopedia of Dance*, Vol. 1 (New York: Oxford University Press, 1999), 358.

10. John Charles Chasteen, *National Rhythms, African Roots: The Deep History of Latin American Popular Dance* (Albuquerque, NM: University of New Mexico Press, 2004), 12.

11. Morales, 12–13.

12. Information for this entry is credited to Vickie Stone at http://www .formedia.ca/rhythms/glossary.html (accessed: March 3, 2010).

13. Ben Sandmel and Rick Olivier, *Zydeco!* (Jackson, MS: University Press of Mississippi, 1999), 22.

14. Morales, 11–14.

15. Moore, 31.

16. Steward, 21, 37.

17. Manuel Peña, "Música Tejana: The Music of Mexican Texas," In Robert Santelli, Holly George-Warren, and Jim Brown Eds. *American Roots Music* (New York: Harry N. Abrams, 2001), 134.

18. Morales, Introduction, xxi.

19. Peña, 138.

20. Sonny Watson's Streetswing.com Archives streetswing.com/histmain/ d5index (accessed: August 8, 2009).

21. http://www.formedia.ca/rhythms/glossary.html (accessed: March 3, 2010).

22. Josefina Ludmer, "The gaucho genre," In *Discovery to Modernism*. Eds. Roberto González Echevarría and Enrique Pupo-Walker. Cambridge University Press, 1996. Cambridge Histories Online. Cambridge University Press. DOI:10.1017/CHOL9780521340694.020 (accessed: May 2, 2010).

23. Peña, 132.

24. http://www.cajundance.com/dances.htm (accessed: April 30, 2010).

Selected Bibliography

Anderson, Jack. *Art Without Boundaries*. Iowa City: University of Iowa Press, 1997.

Aschenbrenner, Joyce. "Dunham Technique Seminars" *Kaiso! Writings by and about Katherine Dunham*. Vè Vè A. Clark and Sara E. Johnson, eds. Madison, WI: University of Wisconsin Press, 2005.

Baim, Jo. *Tango: Creation of a Cultural Icon*. Bloomington and Indianapolis, IN: Indiana University Press, 2007.

Barnes, Denise. "Oh, to Dance: Quite a Feat Classes Tap to the Beat, from Mambo to Modern." *The Washington Times*, September 12, 1996.

Behague, G. *Music in Latin America*. New Jersey: Prentice Hall, 1979.

Benshoff, Harry M. and Sean Griffin. *America on Film: Representing Race, Class, Gender and Sexuality at the Movies*. Malden, MA: Blackwell Publishing, 2007.

Boggs, Vernon W. *Salsiology: Afro-Cuban Music and the Evolution of Salsa in New York City*. Westport: Greenwood Press, 1992.

Chasteen, John Charles. *National Rhythms, African Roots: The Deep History of Latin American Popular Dance*. Albuquerque, NM: University of New Mexico Press, 2004.

Clark, Vè Vè A. "Performing the Memory of Difference in Afro-Caribbean Dance: Katherine Dunham's Choreography, 1938–1987." In *Kaiso! Writings by and about Katherine Dunham*. Vè Vè A. Clark and Sara E. Johnson, eds. Madison, WI: University of Wisconsin Press, 2005.

Daniel, Yvonne. *Rumba: Dance and Social Change in Contemporary Cuba*. Bloomington, IN: Indiana University Press, 1995.

Dávila, Arlene. *Mambo Montage: The Latinization of New York*. New York: Columbia University Press, 2001.

Delgado, Celeste Fraser and José Esteban Muñoz. *Everynight Life: Culture and Dance in Latin/o America*. Durham, NC: Duke University Press, 1997.

Dunham, Katherine. "Negro Dance." In *Kaiso! Writings by and about Katherine Dunham*. Vè Vè A. Clark and Sara E. Johnson, eds. Madison, WI: University of Wisconsin Press, 2005.

"Embrace the Music and Your Partner; Tango's Sexy Form Glides onto D.C. Scene." *The Washington Times*, March 21, 2002, M10.

Flores, Juan. *From Bomba to Hip-Hop: Puerto Rican Culture and Latino Identity.* New York: Columbia University Press, 2000.

Fontyen, Dame Margot. *The Magic of Dance.* New York: Knopf, 1979.

Fortin, Judy. "Zumba Zooms to the Top of the Exercise World." *CNN Health.* September 22, 2008. http://articles.cnn.com/2008-09-22/health/hm.zumba.dance.exercise_1_ alberto-beto-perez-zumba-classes-zumba-fitness?_s=PM:HEALTH.

Giordano, Ralph G. *Social Dancing in America: Lindy Hop to Hip Hop, 1901–2000.* Vol. 2. Westport, CN and London: Greenwood Press, 2007.

Griffin, Al. *"Step Right Up, Folks!"* Chicago, IL: Henry Regnery Company, 1974.

Hodge, Susie. *Dance: Latin and Ballroom.* Chicago, IL: Heinemann Library, 2008.

Jonas, Gerald. *Dancing: the Pleasure, Power, and Art of Movement.* New York: Harry N. Abrams, Inc., 1998.

Lavelle, D. *Latin and American Dances.* London: Pitman, 1975.

Leymarie, Isabelle. *Cuban Fire: the Saga of Salsa and Latin Jazz.* London and New York: Continuum, 2002.

Lipsitz, George. *Time Passages: Collective Memory and American Popular Culture.* Minneapolis: University of Minnesota Press, 2001.

"Losing Louisiana; Zydeco Takes on the World but Is Beaten in the Bayou by Changing Tastes." *The Washington Times,* February 21, 2007, A02.

Macaulay, Alastair. "Twyla Tharp Season With a Cast of Three Companies." *NY Times Dance Review,* October 30, 2007.

Marceau, Yvonne. "Ballroom Dance Competition." In *International Encyclopedia of Dance,* Selma Jeanne Cohen, ed. Vol. 1. Oxford, England: Oxford University Press, 1999.

Marks, Morton. "Brazil, Ritual and Popular Dance." In *International Encyclopedia of Dance.* Selma Jeanne Cohen, ed. Vol. 1. Oxford, England: Oxford University Press, 1999.

Maskosz, Rory. *Latino Arts and their Influence on the United States: Songs, Dreams, and Dances.* Philadelphia, PA: Mason Crest Publishers, 2006.

McDonagh, Don. "Twentieth-Century Social Dance before 1960." In *International Encyclopedia of Dance.* Selma Jeanne Cohen, ed. Vol. 5. Oxford, England: Oxford University Press, 1999.

Moore, Alex. *Ballroom Dancing.* 10th Ed. New York: Routledge, 2005.

Morales, Ed. *The Latin Beat: The Rhythms and Roots of Latin Music from Bossa Nova to Salsa and Beyond.* Cambridge, MA: Da Capro Press, 2003.

Morris, Amy. "Zumba: Newest exercise craze mixes Latin music, dance moves for aerobic workout." April 7, 2008. Available online at http://news.zumba.com/news.

New Grove Dictionary of Music and Musicians. London and Washington, DC: Macmillan Publishers, 1980.

Reynolds, John Lawerence. *Ballroom Dancing: The Romance, Rhythm and Style.* San Diego, CA: Laurel Glen Publishing, 1998.

Rundell, Jennifer. "Let's Zumba." Arlington Heights (IL) *Daily Herald,* September 1, 2008.

"Salsa—It's So Hot . . . They Could Have Been Hosed Down, They Certainly Got Everyone Moving," Coffs Harbour, Australia, *Coffs Coast Advocate,* May 16, 2009, 36.

Sandmel, Ben and Rick Olivier. *Zydeco!* Jackson, MS: University Press of Mississippi, 1999.

Santelli, Robert, Holly George-Warren, and Jim Brown, eds. *American Roots Music.* New York: H. N. Abrams, 2001.

Seigel, Micol. "The Disappearing Dance: Maxixe's Imperial Erasure." *Black Music Research Journal* 25, no. 1/2 (2005).

Shelton, Suzanne. *Divine Dancer: A Biography of Ruth St. Denis.* New York: Doubleday & Company, Inc., 1981.

Sommer, Sally. "Some like It Hot: Salsa Is Spicy, Sexy, and Making Waves in Dance." *Dance Magazine* 78, Issue: 6 (June 2004): 46+.

Sommer, Sally. "Twentieth-Century Social Dance since 1980." In *International Encyclopedia of Dance*, Selma Jeanne Cohen, ed. Vol. 5. Oxford, England: Oxford University Press, 1999.

"Spicing Up Dance Floor with Hip-Shaking Salsa." *The Washington Times*, October 7, 2004, M14.

Stephenson, Richard M. and Joseph Iaccarino. *The Complete Book of Ballroom Dancing.* Garden City, NY: Doubleday & Company, Inc., 1980.

Steward, Sue. *¡Musica!: The Rhythm of Latin America: Salsa, Rumba, Merengue, and More.* San Francisco, CA: Chronicle Books, 1999.

Tharp, Twyla. *Push Comes to Shove: An Autobiography.* New York: Bantam, 1992.

Tomko, Linda. *Dancing Class: Gender, Ethnicity, and Social Divides in American Dance, 1890–1920.* Bloomington and Indianapolis, IN: Indiana University Press, 1999.

Toor, Francis. *A Treasury of Mexican Folkways.* New York: Crown Publishers, Inc., 1979.

"Waterbaby Bagatelles 4/30/1994 premiere company: Boston Ballet." *Abstract.* Available online at http://twylatharp.org/archive/dance_page.asp?dance Selected=101#.

Watson, Sonny. Sonny Watson's Streetswing.com Archives. Available online at http://www.streetswing.com.

Index

About the Author

Elizabeth Drake-Boyt is a theatre and dance historian who gained her PhD in Humanities Interdisciplinary with Performing Arts in May 2005 from Florida State University. Current teaching duties include online theatre and humanities classes through the College of Liberal Arts at the University of Southern Indiana, Evansville, Indiana, and First Year Freshmen Seminar at Pacific University, Forest Grove, Oregon. She has served as director/facilitator of Movement Meditation, which concentrates on expressive dance for non-dancers with fibromyalgia, vertigo, and other disabilities. Publications include more than forty performing arts articles and reviews for *Audience: A Weekly Entertainment Guide* (Boulder, CO), *City Edition* (Denver, CO), *Colorado Daily* (Boulder, CO), *Private Eye* (Salt Lake City, UT), and *Muse* (Colorado Springs/Bouler, CO). Her dissertation was published by DMV Publishing (Germany: May, 2008). Married to Owensboro Public Life Advocate and *Messenger-Inquirer* contributor Charly Wood, Elizabeth is a world-traveler and eternal student.